English for Academic Study

New edition

Writing

Course Book

Anne Pallant

International Study and Language Centre

University of **Reading**

Credits

Published by

Garnet Publishing Ltd.
8 Southern Court
South Street
Reading RG1 4QS, UK

This edition first published 2012

ISBN: 978 1 90861 439 1

British Library Cataloguing-in-Publication Data
A catalogue record for this book is available from the British Library.

Production

Project manager:	Sarah MacBurnie
Project consultant:	Rod Webb
Editorial team:	Claire Forsyth, Fiona Dempsey, Kate Kemp, Fiona McGarry
Art director:	Mike Hinks
Design and layout:	Simon Ellway, Ian Lansley, Maddy Lane
Photography:	Alamy, Corbis, Getty: Keith Brofsky, PhotoAlto/ Sigrid Olsson, David Selman, Jack Star/Photolink, David Sutherland, iStock

Every effort has been made to trace copyright holders and we apologize in advance for any unintentional omissions. We will be happy to insert the appropriate acknowledgements in any subsequent editions.

Printed and bound in Lebanon by International Press: interpress@int-press.com

Acknowledgements

The author and publisher wish to acknowledge the use of material from the following sources:

Buzan, T. (1971). *Speed reading*. Newton Abbot: David and Charles.

Fletcher, K. (2008). *Sustainable fashion and textiles*. London: Earthscan. Retrieved June 6, 2011, from www.earthscan.co.uk. Reprinted with kind permission of Earthscan.

Gladwell, M. (2010). *The Tipping Point: How Little Things Can Make a Big Difference*. London: Abacus.

Gladwell, M. (2004). *Q&A with Malcolm. What is The Tipping Point?* [Promotional interview] Retrieved April 21, 2001, from www.gladwell.com

Godfray, H. C. J., Beddington, J. R., Crute, I. R., Haddad, L., Lawrence, D., Muir, J. F., et al. (2010). Food Security: The challenge of feeding 9 billion people. *Science, 327*(5967), 812–818.

Goldstein, J. S. (1996). *International relations*. New York: HarperCollins.

Held, D., Goldblatt, D., McGrew, A., & Perraton, J. (Eds.). (1999). *Global transformations: Politics, economics and culture*. Cambridge: Polity Press.

Ho, M.-W., & Saunders, P. (2001, July 10). Big business = bad science? *I-sis News 9/10*. Retrieved April 11, 2011, from www.i-sis.org.uk

Marsden, P. (2000). Mental epidemics. *New Scientist, 166*(2237), 46. Retrieved May 9, 2011, from www.newscientist.com. Reprinted with kind permission of New Scientist.

Parkinson, S., & Langley, C. (2009). Stop selling out science to commerce. *New Scientist, 204*(2733), 32–33. Reprinted with kind permission of New Scientist.

Price, A. (2007). *Human resource management in a business context*. (3rd ed.) (pp. 4–9). London: Thomson Learning. Reproduced by permission of Cengage Learning.

Rosenthal, E. (2010, December 11). Using waste, Swedish city cuts its fossil fuel use. *The New York Times* (New York Edition), p. A1. Retrieved May 9, 2011, from www.nytimes.com © *The New York Times*. All rights reserved. Used by permission and protected by the Copyright Laws of the United States. The printing, copying, redistribution, or retransmission of the Material without express written permission is prohibited.

Scullion, H., & Linehan, M. (Eds.) (2005). *International human resource management: A critical text* (pp. 3–10). Basingstoke/New York: Palgrave Macmillan.

Seddon, C. (2011). Lifestyles and social participation. In Beaumont, J.(Ed.). *Social Trends 41* (Newport: Office for National Statistics). Retrieved May 17, 2011 from www.statistics.gov.uk.

Smal, D. (2009, September). *The future of eco-fashion: A design-driven approach*. Paper presented at Fashion: Exploring Critical Issues (1st Global Conference), Oxford. Reprinted with kind permission of the author.

Staff. (2010). Sustainable fashion. *Intelligent Life*, Winter. Retrieved May 19, 2011, from http://moreintelligentlife.com. Reprinted with permission. Copyright © The Economist Newspaper Limited, London.

Staff. (2008, June 7). Telemedicine comes home. *The Economist, 387*(8583), 28–30. Reprinted with permission. Copyright © The Economist Newspaper Limited, London.

c Contents

Acknowledgements

I would like to thank John Slaght for his collaboration on activities linked to the *EAS: Reading* material in the *EAS: Reading & Writing Source Book* for 2012.

I would also like to acknowledge those who have suggested ideas for this edition.

With regard to course content retained from the 2010 edition, many of the principles are based on observations and recommendations made by Ros Richards in her review of the literature.

Thanks also go to the many teachers and students at the International Study and Language Centre (formerly the Centre for Applied Language Studies) who have contributed to the process of trialling and evaluating this material – in particular, Beverley Fairfax, Mary Ferguson, Helen Fraser, Emma Grenside, Belinda Hardisty, Clare McClean, Pete McKichan, Jane Short and Sebastian Watkins. I would like to thank Clare McClean again for her contribution to Unit 2, relating to phrases for making polite suggestions for peer feedback.

Teachers and students of the language centres at the University of Surrey and at Robert Gordon University, Aberdeen, also gave useful feedback.

The author and publisher would like to thank Ron White for his contributions to aspects of the questionnaire on pages 12–15, and for material on comparisons and contrast, adapted from pages 6–9 and 68–69 respectively of White and McGovern (1994).

A particular mention of thanks to all the teachers who taught on the University of Reading Pre-sessional Programme, summer 2011, for their useful comments on the 2012 pilot edition.

Anne Pallant, April 2012

Book map

	Unit	Unit essay	Skills and language focus
1	**Introduction to academic writing** No source text	*(Reflective questionnaire)*	■ Reflecting on the process of academic writing
2	**Sustainable energy** **2a** Using waste, Swedish city cuts its fossil fuel use (1) **2b** Using waste, Swedish city cuts its fossil fuel use (2)	*How can alternative sources of energy be harnessed effectively?*	Getting started: ■ Planning an essay ■ Writing a first draft of an essay ■ Peer evaluation of a first draft ■ Incorporating sources ■ Writing introductions
3	**The business of science** **3a** Stop selling out science to commerce **3b** Is business bad for science?	*Over the past 20 years, commercial influences on scientific research have become increasingly detrimental. Discuss.*	Organizing and supporting ideas: ■ Generating ideas for an essay ■ Organizing ideas ■ Incorporating and referencing sources ■ Using paragraph leaders to help organization
4	**Telemedicine** **4c** Telemedicine	**Timed essay:** *As technology continues to improve, the range of potential uses for telemedicine will increase. Telemedicine will offer more beneficial applications in preventing rather than curing disease. Discuss.*	Writing in examinations: ■ Understanding key instruction verbs in examination questions ■ Interpreting examination questions ■ Writing an examination essay
5	**Food security** **5a** Diet and sustainability **5b** The challenge of feeding 9 billion people **5c** Closing the yield gap **5d** Dealing with the situation	*There are many threats to global food supplies. Explain the problem, identify possible solutions, and assess the implications of implementing these solutions.*	The SPSIE approach to organization: ■ Organizing ideas using the SPSIE approach ■ Concluding sentences in paragraphs ■ Writing conclusions

Unit	Unit essay	Skills and language focus
6 **Human resource management** **6a** Background and origins of people management **6b** International human resource management	*To what extent does human resource management play a formal role in companies?*	Developing your ideas: ■ Analyzing the essay question ■ Writing short definitions ■ Writing extended definitions ■ Paragraph development – exemplification and support ■ Thinking critically ■ Using examples to develop ideas
7 **Sustainable fashion** **7a** Material diversity **7b** Sustainable fashion **7c** The future of eco-fashion: A design-driven approach	*The fashion industry poses a serious threat to the environment. A higher level of sustainability in materials production is the key solution. Discuss.*	Writing about cause and effect: ■ Organizing your essay – cause and effect ■ The language of cause and effect ■ Using statistical facts
8 **The Tipping Point** **8a** The Tipping Point: How Little Things Can Make a Big Difference **8b** Mental epidemics **8c** An interview with Malcolm Gladwell, author of the *The Tipping Point* **8d** *The Tipping Point* by Malcolm Gladwell: Book review **8e** Rumours, sneakers and the power of translation	*Compare and contrast the role of Innovators and Early Adopters with the role of the Early Majority in achieving commercial success. Relate your answer to Gladwell's theory of the Tipping Point.*	Comparing and contrasting: ■ Organizing your essay – comparison and contrast ■ The language of comparison and contrast ■ Incorporating quotations ■ Planning and writing your essay ■ Peer evaluation

i | Introduction

Aims of the course

The purpose of this book is to help you develop the academic writing skills you need to deal effectively with the written element of your academic study, as well as to develop other important skills such as reading research and critical thinking.

Structure of the course

- **Unit structure:** There are eight units in the book. Each unit explores and/or recycles certain key aspects of academic writing, such as organizing and supporting ideas, or writing in examinations. The development of the skills necessary to succeed in these key aspects occurs within the context of a specific topic area, such as *sustainable energy* and *the business of science*. You will have the opportunity to read texts on these and other topics in the accompanying *EAS: Reading & Writing Source Book*. Your writing in any unit will be based on the unit topic. The importance of the context reflects the reality of academic study, where students write about topics and issues within their chosen subject area, and the purpose of writing is directed by the context.
- **Key writing skills:** These are explained where it is felt you need specific information on an area of writing. They usually appear at the end of a task, so that you can reflect on the skills, having done the task.
- **Study tips:** These are included for ease of reference when you are revising what you have studied. They either summarize the outcome of a series of activities, or are a summary of other information contained in the unit.
- **Unit summaries:** Each unit is followed by a unit summary, giving you the opportunity to reflect on what you have learnt.

Additional materials

- **Glossary:** Words or phrases in **bold** (or **bold** and <u>underlined</u> in task instructions) in the text are explained in the glossary on pages 84–85.
- **Peer evaluation sheets:** These can be found on pages 86–91 and provide structured questions to help you evaluate another student's essay and provide useful feedback.

Appendix

The appendix on pages 92–93 contains an *Assessing my progress* form for you to complete once you have finished the course. You should use it to assess the progress you have made on the course, by evaluating the essays you have written and deciding on your strengths and weaknesses.

Working with the course

When you are writing in another language, you not only need to think about the language to express your ideas, but you also need to understand the writing conventions associated with it. This can be particularly challenging with academic writing, where the writing conventions may be very different to the conventions used in your own academic culture. This book will help you in two ways:

- by providing you with guided instruction on what to do and how to do it
- by giving you the opportunity to practise writing in a similar context to the one you will use in your future studies

What you put into the course will determine how much you get out of it. If you want to improve your academic writing, it is essential to practise the skills. You should therefore prepare well for the sessions, as well as participating actively in them.

The process approach to writing

The **process approach** to writing has been widely used for a number of years on writing courses throughout the world. The approach has proved itself an effective way of improving the academic writing skills of students studying English for academic purposes (EAP). The basic concept of this approach is that good writers go through a number of processes while composing a text before they produce their final product. The main underlying principles are:

■ **Writing is a recursive process. Effective writing results from rewriting and revising at each stage of the composing process. A good writer goes back and thinks again before continuing to write. You will be asked to:**
  - **brainstorm** ideas, i.e., think quickly to get ideas for your essay
  - organize your ideas into a plan
  - write your first draft
  - revise and edit your first draft, according to peer feedback and your own developing ideas
  - rewrite it to produce a second draft
  - revise and edit your second draft, according to teacher feedback and your own developing ideas
  - rewrite it to produce a third draft

■ **It helps to share and discuss the writing process with others.** Your work improves if you talk to others about your ideas and problems. Simply by talking to another student, you can clarify aspects of your work that you are not sure about. Another person will have an objective view, as your reader, and will be able to make useful suggestions about your writing. When you write, it is for an audience; you should therefore consider ways of structuring your message so that you communicate your ideas in the clearest way. Showing your writing to others will provide you with feedback on how to adapt your writing to different audiences.

During this writing course, you will have the opportunity to discuss your writing at each stage of the process.

■ **A good writer is critical of his/her own work.** You should read your work carefully and consider both the strengths and weaknesses of your writing.
  a. **Self-evaluation:** To help you develop your critical ability, you will be asked to consider a series of *evaluation questions*, which you will use to evaluate your own writing.
  b. **Peer evaluation:** You will also be asked to consider a series of evaluation questions which you will use to evaluate the writing of another student. You will carry out peer evaluation by reading the student's essay, offering suggestions and comments in a way that is both helpful and constructive. You will then benefit from the comments of the other student. When reading a student's essay, you will focus on the organization of the ideas and the overall argument of the text. At this stage, this is more important than the accuracy of the language, spelling and punctuation, unless errors make the essay difficult to understand.

Your teacher will read the second draft of your essays, and will respond with comments and suggestions. His/her feedback will focus on:
  - task achievement, i.e., how well you have responded to the title of your essay
  - organization and development of ideas
  - content
  - language

He/she will give you feedback on language problems through the use of symbols, which will indicate the type of error you have made, such as:

- using the wrong word (*WW*)
- using the wrong form of the word (*WF*)

Your teacher will explain this system in more detail and refer you to a key to the symbols. You will be asked to correct your language errors, as well as improve other aspects of your essay; this will be your final editing work.

Although some of these approaches may be unfamiliar to you, the aim is to help you acquire skills with which you will be able to produce good written English without dependence on a teacher. This is essential for your future studies.

In diagrammatic form, the process looks like this:

The development of critical thinking skills

At the advanced level necessary for your studies, academic writing should express the **critical thinking** and reasoning that has been used to develop the main ideas in your writing (see *The link between reading and writing* on page 10). This is a fundamental skill which is necessary for successful academic study in higher education. It could typically involve:

- assessing information to show how it relates to an understanding of the *truth* in a particular context
- identifying problems
- seeking solutions to these problems
- evaluating the solutions
- assessing the implications (or effect) if those solutions are applied

Research has shown that working for a period of time on one particular topic provides a basis for developing and expressing critical thinking skills. This is one of the reasons why your writing tasks are based on specific reading texts.

Many of the tasks you will carry out during the course will contribute to the development and expression of your critical thinking skills. You will probably discover that writing of this kind in English higher education differs from writing in your own language.

The microskills of writing

EAS: Writing will also deal with other important aspects of writing, known as **microskills**. These include:

- how to write an effective introduction and conclusion
- how to communicate the main idea of a paragraph to the reader
- how to support your main ideas with examples
- how to express yourself in writing using more complex sentences
- how to write accurately and fluently using language appropriate to the task

The importance of genre

In later units, *EAS: Writing* will look at how different academic subjects require different styles of writing, i.e., **genre**. For example, an essay written in a science subject will typically be in a more **concise** style than one written in a social science subject. A variety of ways of organizing writing will therefore be analyzed and practised. These will include essays of:

- cause and effect
- situation, problem, solution(s), implication(s) and evaluation (**SPSIE**)
- comparison and contrast

The course will also increase your awareness of the most appropriate type of language for expressing these patterns of organization. By the end of the course, you should be able to write effectively for your individual purposes, and be able to make appropriate choices when approaching a writing task. In your writing, you should be able to show clear development of a topic through good organization and language use.

The link between reading and writing

Research has shown that an integrated approach to the teaching of writing contributes to the development of the critical thinking skills of the learner. Carson and Leki view critical thinking as: 'the ability to transform information for their own [students'] purposes in reading and to synthesise their prior knowledge with another text in writing … Together, reading and writing facilitate the development of critical thinking' (1993, p. 100).

The implication of research for teaching academic writing is that there should be an integrated skills approach that includes the specific development of critical thinking skills.

The structure of *EAS: Writing* reflects this approach. Each unit has a writing topic that is based on the relevant reading text in the *EAS: Reading & Writing Source Book*. This follows the principle that, as a student, you read an academic text for a particular purpose. One of the main purposes of the texts will be to provide relevant information to support your ideas in the written assignments. You will need to process and critically analyze that information before incorporating it in your own argument. In this way, you will be engaging in problem-solving activities. It is important that your writing development reflects the problem-solving you will meet in your academic study.

During the course, you will carry out tasks that develop your awareness and skill in incorporating **sources** into your writing; you will learn to **paraphrase** and use quotations, as well as how to acknowledge sources accurately. As the sources you refer to are the ideas of other writers and not your own, it is essential to acknowledge them accurately. Inaccurate referencing can be considered as 'stealing' ideas – known as **plagiarism** – a serious offence in academic life.

Timed writing

Written examinations will be a major method of formal assessment once you start your chosen degree course. To be successful in examinations, you will need the ability to write quickly and concisely when answering a question. Writing to complete an essay within a time limit will be practised on this course as an integral component. You will also develop your technique in quickly analyzing an examination question, in order to respond to the task appropriately.

Some practical points

You should type your first drafts in a word-processing programme. This is because:

- it is easier for your classmates to read
- it is easier to make corrections and revisions to your work
- you will be required to submit word-processed essays in your future studies

You should use an approved university style of layout. This might be Times New Roman font size 12 and 1.5 spacing for the main body of your text. However, if you have little or no experience in word processing, you should discuss with your teacher when you begin typing your essays.

When you give your teacher the second draft of your essay, you will also give him/her your plan and your first draft. This will enable him/her:

- to assess the effectiveness of the process
- to assess your response to evaluation
- to help you further

Similarly, when you give your teacher the third draft of your essay, you will also give him/her your second draft.

Reference

Carson, E. J., & Leki, I. (1993). *Reading in the composition classroom.* Boston, MA: Heinle & Heinle.

1.6 How important are the following when persuading others that your argument is valid? Tick (✔) *H* for High importance, *M* for Medium importance, *L* for Low importance.

Note: You need to persuade people in the *academic community* such as your tutor and examiners.

H M L

☐ ☐ ☐ analyzing questions

☐ ☐ ☐ stating facts

☐ ☐ ☐ reasoning your argument logically from facts

☐ ☐ ☐ explaining key terms

☐ ☐ ☐ using language appropriate to a particular subject area

☐ ☐ ☐ using other points of view to strengthen your argument or research

☐ ☐ ☐ demonstrating the weaknesses of other people's arguments

☐ ☐ ☐ acknowledging the limitations of your own argument or research

☐ ☐ ☐ supporting your argument with examples

☐ ☐ ☐ frequently summarizing your argument

☐ ☐ ☐ referring to well-argued conclusions

1.7 Should you always think of academic writing as communicating with another person? Why/why not?

_____

_____

_____

1.8 What do you focus on when you are working on these areas of a writing task:

1. while you are writing your first draft

_____

_____

2. when you have finished your first draft

_____

_____

_____

3. before you hand in your final draft

_____

_____

_____

1.9 **What type of academic writing have you done in the past?**

_____

_____

_____

1.10 **What difficulties do you have with writing in English or in your own language? Think about ideas, content, grammar, organization, etc.**

_____

_____

_____

1.11 **What do you do when you have difficulties with your writing?**

_____

_____

_____

1.12 **Do you enjoy academic writing? Why/why not?**

_____

_____

_____

Material adapted from:
White, R. V., & McGovern, D. (1994). _Writing_. Hemel Hempstead: Prentice Hall International.
Richards, R. (2001, April). _Presenting critical thinking as a study strategy for UK higher education_. Paper presented at British Association of Lecturers in English for Academic Purposes Conference, University of Strathclyde, UK.

When you have finished the questionnaire, compare your answers with the rest of your group. Discuss your answers and keep notes of the discussion.

1. Do you have similar views and experiences, or are they very different?
2. Are there any general trends in the group?

Note: As you work through further units in this book, you may change your response to some of the answers you have given. It is therefore useful to return to this unit to help you see your development as a writer.

For web resources relevant to this book, see:
www.englishforacademicstudy.com
These weblinks will provide useful introductory information on the topic of academic writing.

2 Sustainable energy

In this unit you will:

- make decisions about what the essay title is asking you to write about
- consider the most appropriate way to organize your ideas
- write an introduction to your essay
- decide what information in a text is useful to support your ideas
- incorporate information from a text into your writing
- acknowledge your sources accurately

Texts — Sustainable energy, Texts 2a–2b (Source Book pp. 8–11)

In preparation for this unit, you should read extracts from *The New York Times* (Texts 2a and 2b in the *EAS: Reading & Writing Source Book*). This will help you identify information that is relevant to the title of your essay, as well as activate ideas from your own experiences.

The tasks in this unit will prepare you to write the following essay:

▶ How can alternative sources of energy be harnessed effectively?

Task 1 — Microskills: Planning your writing

Before you begin writing, you should spend some time:
- deciding exactly what the question is asking you to write about
- generating ideas about the topic by **brainstorming** possibilities
- organizing your ideas into a plan

Some words in essay titles are more important than others because they contain the main ideas of the topic. These words can be called *key words* because they generate the main ideas that you need to include in your essay and, to a certain extent, determine the content of your essay.

> **Study tip**
>
> It is essential that you understand what the essay title is asking you to do. The more time you spend on this at the beginning, the more time you will save when you write your essay. You will work on this further in Unit 3.

1.1 **Read the essay question above and decide which are the key words.**
   a. Discuss your decisions with another student.
   b. Discuss them with the whole group and your teacher.

1.2 **Spend five minutes writing down all the ideas you can think of that are relevant to the essay topic. Write notes, not complete sentences, so that your ideas flow. The order of your ideas is not important at this stage.**

1.3 **Discuss the ideas you have written in Ex 1.2:**
   a. with another student
   b. with the whole group and your teacher

> **Study tip**
>
> Writing down ideas quickly in note form is a very good way of unlocking your understanding. Let your ideas flow and don't try too hard – you will be surprised by what you already know.

1.4   **Decide which ideas you are going to use in your essay. Decide how you are going to organize your ideas.**

Select your ideas by asking yourself the following questions:
- What knowledge about alternative energy do my readers already have?
- What would they be interested in reading about?

1.5   **Organize the ideas you have selected into a logical order:**
- Group together ideas that seem to belong to the same paragraph.
- Think carefully about the best order in which to arrange the paragraphs.

Note: You may wish to develop some of the ideas further or add new ideas.

1.6   **Evaluate another student's plan.**

When you look at your partner's plan, ask yourself:
1. What is the overall idea in the essay?
2. Does the plan follow a logical sequence of ideas?
3. Are the ideas grouped effectively into paragraphs?
4. Is the main idea clear in each paragraph?
5. How many paragraphs will the essay contain?

If the answers to these questions are not clear from looking at your partner's plan, ask him/her to explain. Perhaps the plan needs to be changed or developed more.

> **Study tip**
>
> Writing a clear plan will save you time later.

1.7   **Think about your partner's comments on your plan and try to improve it.**

Write the first draft of your essay.
You should try to write between 400 and 600 words.

Key writing skills: Evaluating a writing plan
Remember your plan is your guide. When you think more about your essay and start to write, you may need to change your plan, so always be prepared to re-evaluate it.

Task 2	Peer evaluation

2.1   **Read and evaluate the first draft of another student's essay.**

When you finish your first draft, exchange it with another student. Read your partner's draft carefully and respond to the questions on the **peer evaluation** sheet for Unit 2 (see page 86). When commenting on your partner's draft, try to use constructive criticism to give feedback and advice.

> **Study tip**
>
> Make sure you benefit from the ideas and opinions of your fellow students. Academic study gives you an opportunity to work together and share ideas.

2.2   **Practise polite ways of providing feedback.**
a. Study the expressions on page 18.
b. Practise using them with a partner to discuss features of essays, as in the examples below.

Examples
Why don't you change this heading?
Maybe it would be better to shorten the introduction?

2.3 Give feedback to your partner based on your comments in the *peer evaluation sheet*.

Giving peer feedback

Phrases for making polite suggestions

Cautious suggestions

It might be a good idea if you …
It might be a good idea to …
Maybe it would be better to …
Do you think a better approach might be to …?

Agreeing, with suggestions

I agree with you, but you could …
Right, but you could …
This is/That's good, but you could …

Straightforward suggestions

Why don't you …?
What about …?
Perhaps you could …
Have you thought about (verb + *ing*) …?

Suggesting alternatives

I think it would be better if you …
Can I make another suggestion?
How about this?

Giving advice

My advice would be to …
I would recommend that you …

Remember that peer feedback should be supportive and helpful, providing constructive criticism. In English culture, it is considered polite to be hesitant about making suggestions. For example, agreeing and then making a suggestion is one way of doing this.

Key writing skills: Giving peer feedback

It is always helpful to get another opinion about your writing. This will not only help you improve your essay writing, but also help you to become used to the idea of modifying and redrafting; this is a key idea in academic study.

| Task 3 | **Microskills: Incorporating other sources into an essay** |

Academic writing can involve:

- reading about a topic
- using ideas from your reading in your writing
- commenting critically on a topic

You have read two texts about how the city of Kristianstad uses alternative energy sources effectively. You should now have an idea about which parts of the texts are useful for your essay, i.e., information that is relevant to the title:

 | How can alternative sources of energy be harnessed effectively?

3.1 **Highlight parts of the text that are relevant. What information from the texts do you want to incorporate into your essay?**

3.2 **Discuss your choice with another student.**

3.3 **Discuss how you will include this information in your essay with your partner.**
You may choose to use different ways of incorporating information.

3.4 **Which of the following from Text 2a are key ideas and which are secondary ideas or examples.**
1. energy sources such as potato peels
2. the heat generated from waste products

Read the information below about creating a hierarchy of ideas.

When you build an argument, it is important to understand the relationships between the different ideas you include. It can help to note them down in diagrammatical form according to whether they are key ideas, secondary ideas or examples.

3.5 **Study the following extract from Text 2a. A student has chosen to use it in his/her essay, as an example of how alternative sources of energy can be used effectively.**

Instead, as befits a region that is an epicentre of farming and food processing, it generates energy from a diverse assortment of ingredients like potato peels, manure, used cooking oil, stale cookies and pig intestines. A massive ten-year-old plant on the outskirts of Kristianstad uses a biological process to transform this detritus into biogas, a form of methane. The gas which is produced is burned to create heat and electricity, or is refined as a fuel for cars. Once the city council got into the habit of harnessing power locally, they began developing fuel from a variety of sources: Kristianstad also burns gas emanating from an old landfill and sewage ponds, as well as wood waste from flooring factories and tree pruning.

Follow the steps below showing how these ideas could be represented in note form.

Step 1: Identify and highlight the key ideas in the text relating to effective use of alternative sources of energy.

Step 2: Select the most important idea and write this at the top of what will become your hierarchy of ideas.

Step 3: Add further points below the most important point, arranging them in order of importance to the argument. The least important idea will be at the bottom of the diagram.

Step 4: Draw lines to show the relationships between ideas and label these lines with a word or phrase that explains the relationship.

Step 5: Check the accuracy of the information in the notes.

Step 6: Incorporate the key concepts and their relationships in a summary of this information, using your own words.

Study tip

This might seem difficult and time-consuming at first, but it is part of the process of joining the academic community. Once you get used to doing this, it will start to seem a normal part of the process.

Use of biofuels in Kristianstad

Most important point: the successful end result of processing the waste products of benefit to humans.

Second most important point: the result of the processing (i.e. the production of biogas).

Third most important point: the original source(s) of the energy.

Fourth most important point: the location of the processing activity.

Note that the examples of the waste (i.e. sources of energy) are not considered important at this stage, so can be noted at the bottom of the page.

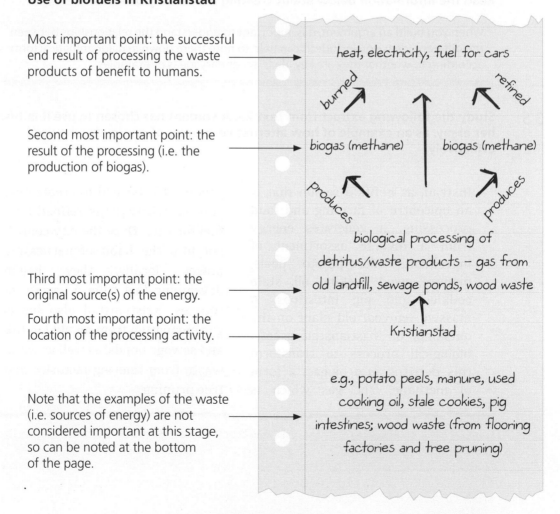

3.6 Complete the summary using the notes in the diagram on page 20.

Waste _____ have been successfully harnessed to provide heat,
_____ and car fuel in Kristianstad, Sweden. Potato peels, used
cooking oil and stale biscuits are some of the discarded products, which
are _____ processed to produce a type of _____
gas, that can either be _____ to produce heat and electricity, or
_____ to produce car fuel. Thus, normal everyday waste can be
an _____ alternative energy source, and should be considered as a
solution to diminishing fossil fuel supplies.

> **Go back to the extracts you have chosen for your essay. Go though the same process with each one to show how you will incorporate them in your essay.**

You now need to acknowledge the source of your information, i.e., say that your information about Kristianstad comes from an article in *The New York Times* by Elisabeth Rosenthal.

If you do not acknowledge your sources, it may seem that you are stealing another person's ideas and claiming them for your own. This is called **plagiarism** and is considered a very serious offence in academic culture.

Study tip

Before you submit your essay, remember to check that you have acknowledged all your sources, both within your essay and more fully at the end. This will help you avoid plagiarism in your writing.

APA referencing system

The way to acknowledge sources accurately is to put the details in the full reference at the end of your essay. For an article on a newspaper's website, this is as shown above. Note that the punctuation is very important.

The above example uses the American Psychological Association (APA) method for giving references, and this system is used throughout this book. Once you start your degree programme, your department may ask you to use a different system. You should always follow the conventions of your academic discipline, or the department in which you are studying, and use them consistently.

As well as giving a full reference for the newspaper article at the end of the essay, you need to acknowledge the source in the body of your essay. This is called in-text referencing or citing. Your teacher will show you one way of citing the information above.

Task 4   Microskills: Writing introductions

A good essay has clear sections, and the first section is the introduction. This is a very important part of the essay as it establishes the relevance and importance of the essay content to the reader.

4.1   **Think about and discuss your own ideas of what to put in an introduction.**

a. Write as many ideas as you can in your notebook.

b. Discuss your ideas with another student and explain the reasons for your choice.

Be prepared to share your ideas in a class discussion.

4.2   **Clarify your understanding of how to write an introduction by answering the following questions.**

1. What function or purpose does the introduction of an essay have?

_____

_____

_____

_____

2. What should an introduction contain?

_____

_____

_____

_____

3. Should an essay always have an introduction?

_____

_____

_____

_____

4.3   **The following four sentences come from the introduction to the essay:**

 What is the most effective way to relieve poverty?

a. *It is clear that it is difficult to find a solution to the issue of poverty, and serious attempts need to be made to tackle this problem.*

b. *This essay will discuss some of the most effective ways to relieve poverty, looking at the reasons why they are successful.*

c. *High levels of poverty have been a cause for concern for many countries for many years.*

d. *It will focus on the development of educational opportunities as being the most successful approach.*

Decide on the most logical order of sentences a–d and complete column 2 of the table.

Order	Sentence	Function
1		
2		
3		
4		

Compare your order with another student and explain your decision.

4.4   **Now decide what the function of each sentence is with your partner.**
Choose functions from the box below and write them in column 3 of the table.

> organizational framework   background statement about the topic
>
> writer's viewpoint (stance)   more specific information on the topic

Note: The writer's viewpoint or stance is also known as the **thesis statement**. The thesis statement is usually one or two sentences presented in the introduction following a general statement about the topic and background information.

4.5   **Read the following five introductions to an essay entitled *What are the most valuable alternative energy sources?***
a. Read carefully and think about your reaction to them.
b. Analyze each introduction and evaluate its strengths and weaknesses.

> 1. There are different alternative energy programmes in different countries. Every country has a programme that is adapted to each country, as some energy sources may not be appropriate in some countries. In Middle Eastern countries the sun is very strong, so there may be projects to use the sun as a source of energy. This essay is about using solar energy in Saudi Arabia, with a focus on cost effectiveness.

2. Viable alternative energy sources are one of the most important goals of many countries. There are some relevant factors to obtain this goal, such as a country's natural resources. This essay will describe some of the energy sources that are relevant to South America, with a particular focus on solar and wind energy as being the most viable.

3. Everybody wishes to see alternative energy sources being used in China, but with so many people, and so much new industry, this is difficult. To be successful, the government needs to harness all possible natural sources of energy. China is a large country, so the possibility is good. Therefore, this essay will describe alternative energy in China and indicate the related factors.

4. Finding alternative energy sources is one of the big projects of the 21st century in all countries. The world is running out of its natural resources. It is important for a country to determine the best way to continue to provide energy for its people. This essay will focus on the development of appropriate alternative energy sources for Thailand, with an emphasis on solar energy.

5. What is the most viable alternative energy source? Many factors to describe it can be found. Its importance depends on the following: a country's natural resources, government policy, the potential market, research systems and facilities. In Japanese society, there is a lot of interest in alternative energy, as there are a great number of people who use energy. So energy has to be cost effective. Therefore, many people spend a lot of time researching this question. This essay discusses ways to develop viable alternative energy sources in Japan, and tries to conclude which could be the most viable.

Source: Edited extracts from authentic student material.

4.6 **Imagine you are writing essays on the following three topics. Write a suitable introduction to each one.**

Note: You are not going to write the whole essay.

 Discuss ways to improve the education system in your country.

 How has technology improved the effectiveness of communication?

The rapid development of electronic communications may mean that people will have fewer social skills. Discuss.

> **Study tip**
>
> Always spend time on your introduction as it plays a crucial role in the essay; it provides the reader with a clear indication of the main areas you are going to discuss.

4.7 **When you write the second draft of your essay** *How can alternative sources of energy be harnessed effectively?* **make appropriate changes to the introduction and other parts according to your peer feedback session.**

Unit summary

In this unit you have thought about the different stages of the writing process and practised planning, writing a first draft and giving peer feedback. You have also looked at how to write effective introductions to your essays, and at incorporating information from sources into your writing.

1 **Match the words and phrases in the box with their definitions below. They are all procedures and techniques that form part of the writing process.**

| drafting | brainstorming | peer feedback |
| organizing ideas | | adopting a critical stance |

a. Generating and noting down initial ideas about a topic without ordering them.

_____

b. Putting ideas together in a logical sequence.

_____

c. Deciding on and expressing your viewpoint after examining and judging possible opinions.

_____

d. The process of writing and putting your essay together. Most essays will have two or more drafts and will be revised and edited after each draft.

_____

e. Comments on your essay from other students.

_____

2 **Complete the sentences below on writing an academic text using some of the words from Ex 1.**

a. When you are given a writing task, it is important to start by _____

_____

b. When you write the first draft, you should _____

_____

c. Before you hand in your final draft, _____

_____

3 **After working on this unit, write down in your notebook ways in which you improved your knowledge of academic writing.**

For web resources relevant to this book, see:
www.englishforacademicstudy.com
These weblinks will provide you with information on organizing ideas in essays, including writing introductions, as well as further reading on sustainable energy.

3 The business of science

In this unit you will:

- make decisions about what the essay title is asking you to write about
- consider the most appropriate way to organize your ideas
- incorporating and referencing sources
- practise writing paragraph leaders

Texts   The business of science, Texts 3a–3b (Source Book pp. 12–16)

In this unit, you will have the opportunity to read two extracts from articles, one from *New Scientist* and another from the *Harvard Business Review* (Texts 3a and 3b in the *Reading & Writing Source Book*).

The tasks in this unit will prepare you to write the following essay:

> Over the past 20 years, commercial influences on scientific research have become increasingly detrimental. Discuss.

Task 1   Microskills: Generating ideas

In this task you will generate ideas, organize your ideas and write a plan. You have already practised doing this in Unit 2, so you will be familiar with the process. Reflect on any improvement you have made at the end of the task.

1.1 **Study the essay title and answer these questions.**
   1. What are the key words in the essay title?
   2. Why do you think they are the key words?

   Discuss your ideas with another student.

1.2 **Write down any ideas you think might be relevant to the essay topic.**
   Write the ideas in the order you think of them in five minutes.

1.3 **Discuss the ideas you have generated in Ex 1.2 with two other students.**
   Decide which ideas are particularly relevant to the topic and the best ones to use in your essay.

1.4 **Read sentences 1–4. Which of them is the essay asking you to do?**
   1. *Explain all the commercial influences on scientific research to your reader.*
   2. *Persuade your reader that commercial influences on research are either damaging or enriching.*
   3. *Write a historical description of all commercial influences on scientific research.*
   4. *Explain to your reader that research has shown there are different commercial influences on scientific research, and persuade him/her that some of these influences are more damaging than others.*

1.5 **Discuss your choice and explain your reasons:**
  a. in groups of three
  b. with the rest of the class

1.6 **What would be an appropriate way to organize your ideas for this type of essay? Why? Discuss your ideas in groups.**

1.7 **Read Texts 3a and 3b to expand your ideas.**
What ideas and information could help you develop your own ideas and provide **academic evidence** to support your argument?

Discuss your thoughts with another student.

> **Study tip**
>
> It is essential that you understand what the essay title is asking you to do. The more time you spend on this at the beginning, the more time you will save when you write your essay. You will work on this further in Unit 4.

Task 2	Organizing ideas in your plan

2.1 **Organize your ideas in a logical essay plan and clearly show the structure of your essay. Use the prompts below to help you.**
  a. Group together ideas which seem to belong to the same paragraph.
  b. Give enough information to show how you will support your ideas.
  c. Think carefully about the order in which you will arrange the paragraphs.

> **Study tip**
>
> Writing a clear essay plan that shows the structure of your essay will save you time later.

2.2 **Evaluate another student's essay plan using these questions as a guide. Then discuss your findings with your partner.**
  1. What is the overall idea in the essay?
  2. Is it obvious from the introduction section what the writer's **thesis** is?
  3. Does the plan follow a logical sequence of ideas?
  4. Are the ideas grouped effectively into paragraphs?
  5. Is the main idea clear in each paragraph?
  6. How many paragraphs will the essay contain?

Note: If the answers to these questions are not clear from looking at your partner's plan, ask him/her to explain. Perhaps the plan needs to be changed or developed further.

2.3 **Consider your partner's feedback on your plan and try to improve it.**

In Unit 2, you looked at ways of incorporating ideas from a text into your writing to support your points. You will now extend this skill by adding comment(s) to support your points further.

For example, if you want to persuade your reader that commercial influences on scientific research are detrimental, you may wish to use the following extract/idea from Text 3a (lines 23–30) to illustrate your point.

> The rapid spread of partnerships between businesses and universities has led to some disciplines becoming so intertwined with industry that few academics are able to retain their independence. Chemical engineering and geology are strongly linked to oil companies, for example, and it is hard to find an engineering department in the UK which does not receive funding from the arms industry.

3.1   **The following notes show the hierarchy of ideas in the extract.**

Complete the notes by referring to the text.

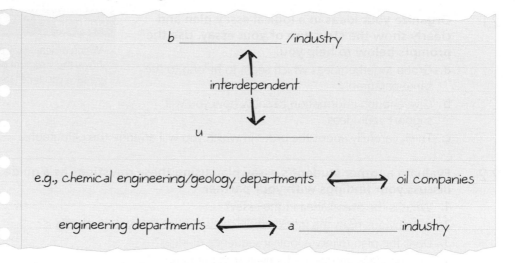

b _____ /industry

interdependent

u _____

e.g., chemical engineering/geology departments ⟷ oil companies

engineering departments ⟷ a _____ industry

3.2   **Use the notes in Ex 3.1 to summarize the information in your own words.**

_____

_____

_____

3.3   **Compare your summary with the one below. How similar is the wording?**

> The marked increase in commercial financing of university departments, as with the oil industry's support for chemical engineering and geology, has led to diminished autonomy among academic staff.

3.4 **Write two types of reference for the source texts you summarized in Ex 3.2:**
a. for the references at the end of your essay
b. as an in-text citation after your summary

3.5 **In academic writing, it is important to *comment* on ideas from sources you have included in your writing. This helps to integrate the ideas of others into your own work.**
Follow steps 1–3 to understand the process of integrating ideas into your work.
Step 1: Read the extract below and underline the writer's comments.

> The marked increase in commercial financing of university departments, as with the oil industry's support for chemical engineering and geology, has led to diminished autonomy among staff (Parkinson & Langley, 2009). It seems that academic researchers are obliged to research areas dictated by the industry concerned – areas which may be different from a researcher's particular interests. Of greater concern perhaps is the example that many engineering departments are funded by the arms industry. Thus, not only are university departments becoming more dependent on industry for funding, with restrictions on the type of research, but a number of departments receive funding from industries that could be seen as ethically unsound.

Step 2: From the text, identify other ideas that the writer has used to strengthen his point.
Step 3: Discuss your ideas with another student.

3.6 **A student has decided to include the example of agricultural science to strengthen his/her point further. Use the steps in Unit 2 Ex 3.5 to provide a summary of the extract below from Text 3a. Then use steps 1–3 in Unit 3 Ex 3.5 to comment on the extract.**

> Another cornerstone of science that is being eroded is the freedom to set the public research agenda so that it serves the public interest. Governments are increasingly focused on delivering competitiveness, and business interests are able to exert pressure on funding bodies through representatives on their boards. As a result, environmental and social problems and 'blue-sky' research commonly lose out to short-term commercial gain. For example, genetics now dominates agricultural science, not least because genetic technologies are highly patentable. This not only dominates privately-funded research, but also steers publicly-funded research away from work that takes a different approach or explores low-tech solutions. As a result, 'low-input' agriculture, which requires minimal use of chemical fertilisers and pesticides and is cheaper and more useful to poorer farmers, is largely overlooked. Similarly, research on how to improve food distribution receives inadequate support.

3.7 Continue to study Text 3a and 3b for more ideas that you can summarize in your essay, with comments to strengthen your argument.

> **Write the first draft of your essay.**
> You should aim to write between 400 and 600 words.

3.8 Read and evaluate the first draft of another student's essay.
When you finish your first draft, exchange the draft with another student. Read your partner's draft carefully and respond to the questions on the peer evaluation sheet for Unit 3 (see page 87).

Task 4 Microskills: Using paragraph leaders

When you are writing, it is useful to think of your audience and how they will make sense of your ideas. Using clear **paragraph leaders** will help the reader follow your essay more easily.

4.1 Look at the following extracts from the article *Stop selling out science to commerce* and underline the key ideas.

> **a.** Over the past two decades, government policy in the US, UK and elsewhere has fundamentally altered the academic landscape in a drive for profit. (Section 1, lines 17–19, page 12)

> **b.** Research is also undermined by misleading messages put out by industry-funded lobby groups. (Section 2, lines 45–46, page 13)

> **c.** Another cornerstone of science that is being eroded is the freedom to set the public research agenda so that it serves the public interest. (Section 3, lines 56–58, page 13)

4.2 Discuss your ideas in Ex 4.1. Then decide what information you might expect to follow each of the sentences:
- **a.** with another student
- **b.** with the whole class

4.3 Each of the extracts in Ex 4.1 is the first sentence of a different paragraph from Text 3a. Look at these three paragraphs in the *Reading & Writing Source Book* and complete activities a–c.
- **a.** Confirm whether you were right about the information that follows the sentences.
- **b.** Decide what function these sentences have within the three paragraphs.
- **c.** Discuss your ideas with another student.

4.4   **Read the following information on paragraph leaders and discuss how it ties in with what you did in Ex 4.1–4.3.**

> **Key writing skills: Paragraph leaders**
>
> The first sentence in a paragraph can be called a *paragraph leader*. One key function of paragraph leaders is to anticipate the ideas that follow. This type of paragraph leader (also called a **topic sentence**) helps the reader to understand the focus and direction of the paragraph.

4.5   **Imagine you are going to write a paragraph on the use of e-mail in companies. Decide which of the following sentences would make a suitable paragraph leader.**

1. *E-mail is useful in the office.*
2. *One of the most useful functions of e-mail is to communicate efficiently with colleagues abroad.*
3. *There are many uses made of e-mail in the office environment; each of these has both advantages and disadvantages attached to it.*

Discuss your answer with another student and give reasons for your choice.

4.6   **Now imagine you are going to write a paragraph on the benefits for international students of studying in a British university. Decide on the most suitable paragraph leader.**

1. *Studying in a British university is useful for many reasons.*
2. *Studying in a British university provides students with a number of benefits.*
3. *International students prefer to study in the UK.*

Discuss your answer with another student and give reasons for your choice.

> **Study tip**
>
> It is useful to think of paragraph leaders as a way of helping you make your essays more organized and easier for the reader to follow.

4.7   **The paragraph leaders have been removed from the following two paragraphs. Read and decide on a suitable paragraph leader for each one.**

1.

_____

_____

Since English has become the most widely used international language in most fields, many employers require their employees to have a high level of English. It is especially useful for those in academic posts, as so many academic papers are published in English. Those working in financial markets also need English in order to be able to talk to their English-speaking clients and to work effectively in the international market. Other fields for which it is useful to know English include business, commerce and diplomacy. Thus, one of the advantages of being competent in the English language is that there is a wider range of career opportunities.

2.

The first option of building more roads needs to be examined very carefully, as one of the possible effects of further construction is an increase in the volume of traffic, which happened when the motorway around London was built. The second option, that of limiting the number of cars on the road at one time, will not meet with the approval of the general public. The third option, that of providing a more extensive, more efficient and cheaper transport system, seems to be the most viable one. It would encourage people to leave their cars at home, as they would benefit more from using public transport. So the third option should be examined in more detail in order to establish a new system.

Sources: Edited extracts from authentic student material.

> **Make appropriate changes to your essay for Unit 3, taking into account the work you have done on paragraph leaders in Task 4.**

Unit summary

In this unit you have worked on developing skills necessary for organizing your ideas. You have also looked at using paragraph leaders to indicate the topic of the paragraph and link it to previous and subsequent ideas.

1 **Think about the activities you have worked on in this unit and the skills you have practised. Complete the following table with the appropriate activity number.**

Skill	Task/activity
Deciding what the essay is asking you to write	
Deciding the most appropriate way of organizing your ideas	
Deciding what information in a text is useful to support your ideas	
Incorporating that information in your writing	
Effectively introducing your reader to the main idea in each paragraph	

2 **Complete the list of activities below with words and phrases from the box.**

> develop   discuss   group   plan   first draft   key words   relevant
>
> academic evidence   related ideas   paragraph leader   general statements

Organizing your ideas for an academic essay:

Planning a. Identify the _____ in the essay title.

b. Quickly write down all the ideas you can think of that may be _____ to the topic.

c. _____ with other students what the essay is asking for.

d. Read texts on the topic to help _____ your own ideas and provide _____ for your opinions.

Drafting e. _____ your ideas so that _____ are all in the same paragraph.

f. Introduce the topic with _____ and gradually become more specific.

g. Read and comment on another student's _____ or _____.

h. Make sure that you include a clear _____ at the start of each paragraph.

> For web resources relevant to this book, see:
> **www.englishforacademicstudy.com**
> These weblinks will provide you with information covering all aspects of academic writing, including incorporating and referencing sources.

4 Telemedicine

In this unit you will:

- understand the differences between writing an essay in an examination and writing a course assignment
- learn how analyze the essay question quickly
- make decisions about the most appropriate way to organize your ideas
- complete an essay within a time limit

Writing essays under examination conditions is an important aspect of academic study. This unit will help you understand the differences between writing in examinations and writing a course assignment.

Task 1 | Writing in examinations

1.1 **Think about your own experiences of writing an essay in an examination. Then answer questions 1–3.**

1. What is the first thing that you do?

   _____

   _____

2. What is the second thing that you do?

   _____

   _____

   _____

3. What are the next stages that you go through?

   _____

   _____

   _____

Discuss your ideas with another student.

1.2 **Write down three differences between writing an examination essay and a course assignment.**

1. _____

   _____

2. _____

   _____

3. _____

   _____

Discuss your ideas with another student.

1.3 **Complete the table by ticking (✔) the appropriate box, to show which stages in the process of writing academic essays apply to examinations and which apply to course assignments.**

Stage in the process	Writing in examinations	Course assignments
1. Analyzing the title		
2. Brainstorming ideas		
3. Organizing your ideas/plan		
4. Self-evaluation		
5. Peer evaluation		
6. Writing a first draft		
7. Revising your draft		
8. Writing a second draft		
9. Teacher evaluation/ feedback		
10. Evaluation of teacher feedback		
11. Revising your second draft		
12. Writing a third draft		
13. Writing a final draft		

Discuss your views with your partner.

Key writing skills: Stages in examination writing

As you have seen, writing essays in examinations is similar to writing course assignments in a number of ways, but there are some differences. The main difference is the *time constraint*: in an examination you do not have time to completely revise your essay in a second draft. However, you should always leave five or ten minutes at the end of the examination to check your work for spelling and grammar mistakes, and also to add any information you feel will improve your answer.

Despite the time constraint, it is important that you spend time:

■ *analyzing* the title for key words and identifying exactly what the essay requires you to do (two or three minutes). The wording is chosen very carefully by the examiners to get an appropriate answer.

■ *brainstorming* your ideas (about three minutes)

■ *organizing* your ideas into a plan (about five minutes)

Remember: As you do not have time to write more than one draft of your examination essay, it is important to have a good plan to guide you in the structure and direction of your argument.

Task 2 — Key words in examination questions

An important step in analyzing questions is to understand the meaning of key words because they have very specific meanings in the context of examination questions. Questions often have 'instruction' verbs which help you decide your approach.

2.1 **Match the following groups of words to their definitions by writing in the spaces provided.**
Use this exercise to gain a thorough understanding of these words. They will remain a very useful resource throughout your study.

| define | describe | outline | state | summarize |

1. give an explanation of something in detail, e.g., how it works _____

2. give an explanation of the meaning of a term _____

3. sum up something clearly _____

4. provide the main ideas _____

5. convey the main points of a topic _____

| analyze | evaluate | compare | contrast | discuss |

6. detail all the different aspects of an issue or statement, including reasons for your particular viewpoint and evidence to support it _____

7. consider very carefully; examine to find out what something consists of

_____

8. describe the main aspects of two or more things to show their similarities

_____

9. describe the main aspects of two or more things to show their differences

_____

10. detail something's strengths and weaknesses, advantages and disadvantages, and importance _____

| account of/for | comment (on) | consider | prove | explain |

11. describe/give reasons for something _____

12. describe and say what you think about something _____

13. give reasons for; describe a process clearly _____

14. demonstrate that something is true _____

15. give your views on something; say what you think about something – this is often used with a quotation with which you should agree or disagree _____

identify	illustrate	apply(to)	relate	support

16. use examples for clarification _____

17. name and discuss in detail _____

18. use examples to back up a statement or argument _____

19. put something to use; show how something, e.g., a theory, certain findings, data, research results, can be used in a particular situation _____

20. show the connection between two or more things _____

Source: Adapted from Wallace, M. J. (1980). *Study skills in English*. Cambridge: Cambridge University Press. Braine. G., & May, C. (1996). *Writing from sources*. Mountain View, CA: Mayfield.

Task 3	**Interpreting example examination questions**

The essay questions that follow come from genuine past examination papers. By analyzing the questions, you will develop a better understanding of what the examiner wants you to do. For example, does the examiner want you to describe a process or compare two viewpoints?

3.1   Read the questions and decide what each one is asking you to do.

Food science

1. a. What properties do microorganisms have which make them a major cause of food spoilage?

b. Explain what you mean by food spoilage and describe the mechanisms by which microbes cause food spoilage.

c. How, in practice, may microbial food spoilage be reduced or prevented?

Animals in agriculture

2. Discuss reasons why keeping livestock may be particularly important to the welfare of the poorest people in developing countries.

3. Define what is meant by 'breed' in domestic animals. Genetic change in a population may be achieved by breed substitution, crossbreeding and within-breed selection. Define these terms, giving examples.

4. Compare and contrast the characteristics of typical feed resources for ruminant and non-ruminant livestock. Bearing in mind these different feed resources, why does current thinking predict a major expansion for non-ruminant animals in the next 20 years?

Politics of the international political economy

5. Free trade is essential for international economic growth. Discuss.

6. International aid is the key to global development. Discuss.

7. Does the prevailing structure of north–south relations prevent the effective development of the less-developed countries?

Advanced software engineering

8. a. Software quality systems usually contain quality control, quality assurance and quality management components. Give a brief explanation of the need for these three components and examples of their usage.

   b. Discuss the role and importance of software inspection for quality systems.

   c. Explain how 'quality standards' relate to software quality systems.

Horticulture

9. What techniques can be used to minimize the wastage of irrigation water in horticultural production?

Animal sciences

10. Write an essay entitled: 'Ecological implications of global warming'.

Economics

11. The best way to promote human development is to promote economic growth. Discuss.

12. a. Markets are efficient. Discuss.

   b. To what extent is your answer to 12a relevant to events observed in financial markets since 2008?

Finance

13. Explain why you agree or disagree with the view that codes of ethics promote ethical behaviour among employees in the financial services industry.

3.2 **Discuss your ideas with another student or in groups of three.**

3.3 **Choose one of the questions and go through the process of:**
analyze → brainstorm → plan

Text	Telemedicine, Text 4c (Source Book pp. 25–27)

In preparation for this task, you should read the article *Telemedicine comes home* from *The Economist* (Text 4c in the *Reading & Writing Source Book*).

Task 4   Writing your essay

You will find the nine points in Ex 4.1 useful when writing under examination conditions. Although you are not working under these conditions, you should try to relate the advice to your experience of taking examinations.

4.1   **Read the following examination tips and identify the ones you do already. Then discuss with another student how the other points could help you when working under examination conditions.**

Writing in an exam

1. Read the question very carefully. Underline key **terminology**; this will help you understand the type of answer required.
2. Brainstorm the topic; quickly write down every idea you have that could be relevant to the question.
3. Read the question again to check you haven't forgotten anything. Evaluate your ideas, crossing out irrelevant ones.
4. Organize relevant ideas in a plan.
5. Write your answer, starting with a very brief introduction; this should contain a thesis statement that responds to the question and anticipates the main ideas of your answer.
6. Divide your essay into paragraphs, each beginning with an appropriate paragraph leader; this should link to the main idea in your paragraph.
7. Support your paragraph leaders with details and examples.
8. Use linking words to guide the reader through the essay.
9. Leave five to ten minutes at the end to re-read your essay for clarity of ideas, spelling and language.

> **Study tip**
>
> Use your time efficiently during examinations, and make sure you leave time to check your work.

4.2   **Study the essay title, then consider the questions.**
1. What are the key ideas?
2. What is the question asking you to do?

 As technology continues to improve, the range of potential uses for telemedicine will increase. Telemedicine will offer more beneficial applications in preventing rather than curing disease. Discuss.

Discuss your ideas with another student.

4.3   **Brainstorm ideas for this essay by noting down any thoughts you have on the topic.**
To stimulate your thoughts further, you can refer to the article *Telemedicine comes home* in the *Reading & Writing Source Book*.

4.4   **Organize your ideas into a plan.**

Write your essay.
You should be able to write at least 400 words.

Unit summary

In this unit you have practised using essay-writing skills (such as analyzing questions and organizing ideas) within a time limit.

1 **Think about the questions below and write brief answers.**

  a. How is the process of writing in examinations similar to that of writing extended course assignments?

  _____

  b. What can you do in examinations in place of writing a second draft?

  _____

  c. What do you need to look for and highlight when you read the essay title?

  _____

  d. What should you include in your introduction?

  _____

  e. What do you need to check for before handing in your work?

  _____

2 **Complete the essay titles with verbs from the unit. There may be several different possibilities for each title.**

  a. It has been claimed that microwave radiation from mobile phones 'may cause serious diseases and disturbances in the physiology' (Carlo, 2002). _____ this statement and _____ the evidence that supports or contradicts it.

  b. Are mobile phones essential or dangerous? _____ the arguments for and against the use of mobile phones.

  c. Wireless networking and Bluetooth: _____ the characteristics of each and _____ their performance and functions.

3 **Choose three or four more verbs from Task 2 and write more essay titles in your notebook using them.**

For web resources relevant to this book, see:
www.englishforacademicstudy.com
These weblinks will provide you with help in interpreting examination questions and other aspects of understanding writing assignments.

5 Food security

In this unit you will:

- make decisions about what the essay title is asking you to do, and organize your ideas
- consider one approach to problem-solving in your writing
- learn how to end a paragraph with an effective concluding sentence
- practise effectively writing a conclusion

Texts Food security, Texts 5a–5d (Source Book pp. 28–39)

In this unit you will have the opportunity to read a variety of extracts on the topic of food security (Texts 5a–5d in the *Reading & Writing Source Book*). They will provide you with useful background information for your essay.

Task 1 Microskills: Organizing your essay – SPSIE

An important aspect of academic life is *problem-solving*. Whichever subject you study, you will encounter problems that need dealing with. These need critical analysis and evaluation in order to find appropriate solutions. You will be expected to express your analysis in both spoken and written form.

One common approach to problem-solving in academic life involves:

- *examining* the problems that have arisen from a specific situation
- *suggesting* solutions to the problems
- *looking* at the implications of the suggested solutions
- *evaluating* the solutions

When expressing this approach in writing, you need to choose the most appropriate way of organizing your information and the most appropriate language to express your ideas. You will explore these two areas in this unit.

The diagram in the box shows how this problem-solving approach, referred to using the acronym **SPSIE**, is reflected in the organization of text.

Situation ▶ **P**roblems ▶ **S**olutions ▶ **I**mplications ▶ **E**valuation
(SPSIE)

1.1 **Analyze how this organization has been applied in the following sample text.**

I am an international student living in Britain. I find it very difficult to meet British students and so cannot make British friends and practise my English. I will join some university clubs so as to meet some students. Although this will take a lot of my time, it should help me make friends and improve my English.

1.2 Think of a situation you have experienced which has led to a problem (different from the example in Ex 1.1). Write a short paragraph that:

1. introduces the situation
2. explains the problem
3. suggests a solution
4. states the implications
5. evaluates the outcome

Study tip

As you gain experience in writing essays, you will find it easy to use different models of organization.

1.3 **Key writing skills: SPSIE approach to writing**

It is important to consider accepted patterns of organizing your academic writing. The SPSIE model is used widely for texts that explore problems and possible solutions. However, most written texts use a *mixture* of different organizational patterns. Once you have encountered other patterns, you should start using more than one pattern within an essay.

The SPSIE approach can be used for:

- a paragraph
- a section of a longer document
- a complete article
- a complete book

Read the article about global migration. Identify how the pattern described in Ex 1.1 is used in this text.

GLOBAL MIGRATION

The movement of populations across borders has increased to such an extent as to produce a global migration crisis. As a result of this development, a number of ethical issues have arisen relating to issues such as the proportion of ethnic groups within a country; the national identity of a country; racism; the effect of a multicultural society and the distribution of wealth. It is mainly the governments of the host countries that seek to solve these problems by establishing language programmes, cultural-exchange and awareness-raising programmes and, where possible, employment opportunities. However, if this pattern of migration continues, there needs to be more openness and willingness on behalf of the native population to accept and receive migrants into their society, and to realize the benefits that a multicultural society can bring. The implications of this suggestion are wide, and not without problems: many older people are resistant to change, and the working population is resistant to outside competition for employment opportunities. There also needs to be a much higher level of cooperation between the host country and the country of origin in order to establish a clear identity for the migrants.

> It is obvious that any solution to the problems mentioned above will involve much greater cooperation at the levels of citizens, ethnic groups and political bodies; it will also take many years for any adjustment to take place. However, it is hoped that over time and with greater understanding of the global picture and the possibility of a global governing body that is fair to all global citizens, the problems resulting from the issues of global migration will be minimized.

1.4 **Complete the flow diagram using information from the text in Ex 1.3. Write in note form as in the example.**

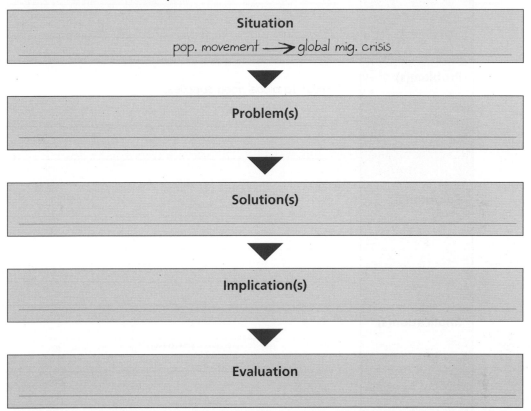

Situation

pop. movement ⟶ global mig. crisis

Problem(s)

Solution(s)

Implication(s)

Evaluation

Compare your answers with another student.

1.5 **Re-read the text and think about the proposed solution. Could it create a further problem?**

1.6 **What language do you think it is appropriate to use when giving an evaluation?**

Task 2	**Writing your essay**

In this unit, you will prepare an essay on the following topic. To support your ideas, you should make particular reference to Texts 5a–5d.

 There are many threats to global food supplies. Explain the problem, identify possible solutions, and assess the implications of implementing these solutions.

2.1 **Read the title carefully and decide on the key ideas.**
Then discuss your views with another student.

2.2 **Make notes on any ideas you have that are relevant to this essay.**
To support your ideas, you should refer to Texts 5a–5d.

2.3 **Discuss your ideas in small groups and then complete the chart below.**

Situation	
Problem(s)	Threat to global food supplies.
Solution(s)	
Implication(s)	
Evaluation	

2.4 **Use the ideas you generated in Ex 2.2 and 2.3 to write a logical plan. This should clearly show the structure of your essay.**

2.5 **Read and evaluate another student's plan. Ask yourself the following questions to help you evaluate his/her plan.**

1. What is the overall idea in the essay?
2. Is it obvious from the introduction section what the writer's thesis is?
3. Does the plan follow a logical sequence of ideas?
4. Are the ideas grouped effectively into paragraphs?
5. Is the main idea clear in each paragraph?
6. How many paragraphs will the essay contain?

If the answers to these questions are not clear from looking at the plan, ask your partner to explain. Perhaps the plan needs to be changed or developed further.

2.6 **Exchange views with your partner on each other's plan. Consider your partner's comments and try to improve your plan.**

2.7 **Write the first draft of your essay.**

2.8 **Read and evaluate the first draft of another student's essay.**
When you finish your first draft, exchange the draft with another student. Read your partner's draft carefully and respond to the questions on the peer evaluation sheet for Unit 5 (see page 88).

| Task 3 | Microskills: Writing concluding sentences |

3.1 **Read the following four paragraphs. What is the function of the final sentence in each paragraph?**

> 1. The rapidity or velocity of migration can be assessed in two ways. First, the movement of people across regions in given time periods can be considered, assessing the length of time a mass migration takes from its inception to its conclusion. Second, velocity in individual terms can be considered – the amount of time it takes a migrant to get from his or her original locale to a new host country. Clearly, changes in transportation technology have made a major difference in this respect. (p. 284)

> 2. Trade, in the sense of the exchange of goods and services between people over distance, has a long history. Great trading empires have arisen periodically ever since regular long-distance travel became possible. But international trade, the exchange of goods and services between nations, by definition only emerged with the establishment of the nation state. Trade has been entwined with the rise of the modern state and its fortunes: states required revenues, above all to wage military campaigns, and trade offered an obvious source of funds. Identifying historical patterns of trade globalization is the primary objective of this chapter, and this entails deploying the analytical framework developed in the introduction. (p. 149)

3. Rapid demographic growth is a key factor in explaining the increasing immiseration of sub-Saharan Africa and processes of desertification and soil decline. This has contributed to the growing economic problems of the region and its mounting international debts. Thus, environmental problems in single African states have spilt over into the international politics of banking. The resolution of these international issues has involved political contests and struggles between Western governments and their financial sectors. In the future, the demographic and environmental squeeze on the South may contribute towards political instability and outward migration, both of which will affect a widening pool of other nations, internationally and domestically. (p. 379)

4. In the last 20 years, a series of technological and political changes have transformed the televisual landscape and have contributed to the globalization of television as a medium and as an industry. First and foremost, the number of countries with broadcasting systems and the number of televisions available on which to watch their output has steadily risen. From its Western core, television has spread in the post-war years across Eastern Europe and the Soviet Union, into Latin America, Asia and Africa.

Second, first within the West, but later in other areas as well, the number of terrestrial channels has steadily climbed. In part, this has been because governments have been prepared to enlarge the funding base for television companies, for there is clearly a limit to the numbers of channels and programmes that can be funded by subsidy/licence fee alone. By allowing advertising revenue and sponsorship into the television funding mix – be it through public corporations taking advertising or wholly private stations – the potential output and funding base of national TV has risen. However, the expansion of output has rarely, if ever, been matched by a corresponding increase in the capacity of national audiovisual industries to supply all of the potential broadcast slots. Thus, the expansion of television output across and within countries has fuelled the demand for television imports. (p. 357)

Source: Adapted from Held, D., Goldblatt, D., McGrew, A., & Perraton, J. (Eds.). (1999). *Global transformations: Politics, economics and culture.* Cambridge: Polity Press.

Discuss your ideas on the function of the final sentences with another student.

3.2 **The concluding sentence in a paragraph can have a number of functions. Complete the following list with some ideas of your own. Then discuss them with your teacher.**

Study tip

Carefully constructed paragraphs not only help your reader, but will also encourage you to think through your ideas in more depth.

The concluding sentence in a paragraph can:

- summarize the main ideas of your paragraph _____
- _____
- _____
- _____
- _____

3.3   Discuss with your class and teacher whether the concluding sentences in the paragraphs in Ex 3.1 have any of the functions you listed in Ex 3.2.

3.4   The concluding sentences in the following paragraphs from student essays have been removed. Write a suitable sentence for each paragraph.

1. Global warming has had a number of negative effects on the environment. Agricultural crops have been damaged; for example, last year's rice production decreased, so many people are suffering from famine. Many African countries, especially, have a much lower yield of agricultural production. Furthermore, the sea levels are rising around the world, which has led to the disappearance of many islands. Global warming can also affect people's health, in particular, extremely hot temperatures can increase the number of people who die on any given day. In hot weather the heart needs to work harder, for example. The weather can also affect the immune system.

   _____

   _____

   _____

2. There are two major reasons for the fall in the quality of teaching. One problem is the pressure of the increasing population on the demand for school places. This situation has placed excessive strain on the system as it tries to meet these demands, and it has also led to a decline in the quality of teaching. As a result, although a large proportion of students may enter the school system, only a small percentage proceed to high school level, and an even smaller number finish high school. The other reason is that teachers' salaries are low. Watson (1980) states that 'teachers in Thailand remain ill paid'; until more money can be injected into teachers' salaries, thereby attracting better staff, the quality of teaching will remain low, and continue to be one of the causes of poor performance by students.

   _____

   _____

   _____

3. The development of information technology has meant that many businesses have been able to reduce their running costs. This revolution has helped reduce the need for paper-handling operations and other routine work. Moreover, it has also enabled companies to dismantle their main offices, and thus cut overhead costs, as many employees can now work at home or in satellite offices, using computers and telecommunication devices.

   _____

   _____

   _____

Sources: Edited extracts from authentic student material.

| Task 4 | **Microskills: Writing your conclusion** |

4.1   **What is the function of the concluding paragraph of an essay?**

_____

_____

_____

_____

_____

Discuss your ideas with another student.

4.2   **Read the following three concluding paragraphs and identify their functions. Each conclusion comes from an essay with this title:**

 Is it better to help developing countries to help themselves than to give them food and machinery?

1. It seems that in countries with misguided policies, where conventional aid is known to fail, those who want to help should concentrate not on lending money, but on the policy of education. They should advise the governments and help to provide different kinds of training; they should act as vehicles for transferring knowledge. Other types of aid are not useful, as they often support the ineffective economic policies of a government, increase a country's dependence on aid, and contribute to a waste of money on projects that are not viable. In some cases, the consequences of such aid are not prosperity and economic development, but stagnation and an increase in poverty. Before giving financial aid or machinery, the people should be educated in how best to use them, which is the most useful contribution developed countries can make to developing countries.

2. To conclude, it is important to stress that developing countries need help, but it is difficult to decide which is the most effective and appropriate help for any given situation. The countries which want to help are wise to include local people in the early stages of planning an aid project, as this cooperation results in the continuity of the programme, and ongoing interest in and maintenance of the project over a long period. So a logical outcome of viewing development aid as a right and not as a gift, is that development cooperation should be based on a genuine partnership, with programme ownership and implementation anchored in the developing countries. However, in spite of all these possible solutions, it is the responsibility of developing countries to choose the best way, because they know their own situation. They need only to be shown the direction in which to go in order to solve their problems, and then they will be able to achieve their goal.

3. In conclusion, it seems that the roots of the current crisis from which the Third World suffers are centuries old, as some of them date from the 19th century and are directly linked to colonialism. In spite of all the efforts that have already been made in the economic and social fields, the problems still exist. If no action is taken within the next few years, the situation will inevitably deteriorate and even affect the interests of the developed countries, as they will lose the extensive markets that the developing countries represent.

Sources: Edited extracts from authentic student material.

Key writing skills: Writing conclusions

A conclusion should signal to your readers that you have finished your writing and leave them with the clear impression that you have achieved the purpose(s) of your essay. Conclusions typically include:

- a summary of the main points (but be careful not to repeat exactly what you have already written)
- concluding statements drawn from the points you made in the main body
- suggestions or recommendations for action to be taken
- predictions formed from information in the main body

The conclusion should *not* include any new important ideas. Such ideas should have already been discussed in the main body. An effective conclusion will often progress from a *specific statement* to a *general statement.* Note that this is the opposite progression to that of an effective introduction, which progresses from a general statement to a specific thesis statement.

4.3 **The following three sentences come from a conclusion to an essay entitled *The benefits of higher education*. Number the sentences in the most logical order.**

1. In that sense, educational levels are likely to be improved and education methods become more efficient. ☐

2. To conclude, it seems that universities and higher education establishments have been of widespread importance in the improvements and developments realized in modern societies. ☐

3. However, more should be done to ensure further improvement and participation of those bodies in the development process, for instance the cancellation of tuition fees, or at least a reduction. ☐

Sources: Edited extracts from authentic student material.

4.4 **Compare your order with that of another student and explain your choice. Then identify the function of each sentence.**

4.5 The following extracts from the conclusion of an essay entitled *The consumption of tobacco and its consequences* are in the wrong order. Number them in the most logical order.

1. However, most people recognize that many developed countries use the international organizations as a curtain to achieve their purposes. This is because they are by far the biggest beneficiaries of tobacco production, gaining $100 billion a year from taxes on tobacco. ☐

2. A rational consideration of this situation should lead to a ban on tobacco consumption being introduced, resulting in fewer deaths from smoking-related illness. However, there are many who believe that, despite repeated efforts to instigate change, the present situation will remain indefinitely. ☐

3. We have established that there are so many possible solutions to the problems of tobacco consumption that it would be impossible to consider them in an essay of this length. ☐

4. As discussed in this paper, tobacco companies often respond to tobacco problems by suggesting solutions that benefit their own interests, rather than those of the developing countries, and use international organizations to introduce them. ☐

Sources: Edited extracts from authentic student material.

4.6 Look carefully at the conclusion of your essay on global food supplies and revise it according to the tasks that you have completed in Unit 5.

Key writing skills: Concluding paragraphs

The concluding paragraph of an essay provides a similar function to a concluding sentence in a paragraph:

- The concluding *sentence of a paragraph* can summarize the *main idea of a paragraph*.
- The concluding *paragraph of an essay* can summarize the *main ideas of the essay*.

Human resource management

Unit summary

In this unit you have focused on how to organize your ideas in a situation–problem–solution–implication–evaluation (SPSIE) pattern. You have also looked at the functions of concluding sentences and paragraphs.

1 At the beginning of this unit you read that the unit would help you develop four specific skills. Look back and decide at what stage in the unit you practised these. Complete the following table with the appropriate activity number.

Skill	Task/activity
a. Make decisions about what the essay title is asking you to do, and organize your ideas.	
b. Consider one of the ways to approach discussions of problems in your writing.	
c. Learn how to end a paragraph with an effective concluding sentence.	
d. Practise effectively ending an essay with a conclusion.	

2 Think about the microskills you have learnt in this unit. Then complete a–d with your own ideas. You may wish to use some of the words in the box.

complete	appropriate	function	evaluate	accurate	signal
specific	general	implications	new	ideas	

a. Each paragraph in an academic essay should have a concluding sentence which _____

_____

_____

b. If you are discussing solutions to problems, you should _____

_____

c. The conclusion to your essay should _____

_____

d. It should not _____

_____

For web resources relevant to this book, see:
www.englishforacademicstudy.com
These weblinks will provide you with further help with organizing your ideas, with more information about the SPSIE approach and with writing conclusions.

Human resource management

In this unit you will:

- practise writing short and clear definitions
- write extended definitions
- develop your skill in supporting and exemplifying your ideas

Texts	Human resource management, Texts 6a–6b (Source Book pp. 40–44)

For the essay in this unit, you will read extracts from two books on human resource management (Texts 6a and 6b in the *Reading & Writing Source Book*).

Identify information that is relevant to the title of this essay:

 To what extent does human resource management need to play a formal role in companies?

Use the techniques you have learnt in Units 2–5 to plan your essay for this unit.

Task 1	**Analyzing the question**

You have already done some work on analyzing the question. You can continue to put into practice all you have learnt so far.

1.1 **Read the essay title above.**
  1. How many parts to the title are there?
  2. What are the key ideas in the essay title?

  Discuss your ideas with another student.

1.2 **What kind of organizational structure would be appropriate for this title?**

1.3 **Write down any ideas you think might be relevant to the essay topic in five minutes.**

  Use notes and write them in the order you think of them.

Task 2	**Microskills: Writing short definitions**

Definitions are an important component of academic essays. You will now look at how to write definitions in the context of academic writing.

2.1   **Think about the following definition of a teacher.**
A teacher is a person who teaches.
1. Is it a suitable definition?
2. If it is, why? If it is not, why not?

Discuss your ideas with another student.

2.2   **Discuss with your partner when and why you need to define a word or terminology in academic life.**
Think about this in a variety of contexts, spoken as well as written.

2.3   **Study these words and the context in which they are being used. Which words do you think need a definition, and why?**

Word	Context
1. gene	You are a genetic engineer writing an article for a biotechnology journal.
2. nurture	You are a pre-sessional student writing for a non-specialist readership.
3. migration	You are a sociologist writing a first-year undergraduate textbook.
4. education	You are a pre-sessional student writing an essay on which form or forms of education contribute to the social and economic development of a society.
5. globalization	You are a university lecturer writing an article on the impact of economic globalization on developing countries for an international relations journal.
6. particle physics	You are a journalist writing an article for a quality newspaper.
7. desertification	You are a geography lecturer writing a university textbook about the changing climate in Central Africa.
8. skimming	You are an English-language teacher writing a book on how to read efficiently.

2.4   **Discuss your ideas with your partner. Try to reach agreement about the reasons for your choices.**
Note: The amount and nature of the information that a writer gives in a definition will depend on:
- whether the concept is considered to be new for the readers
- how much knowledge of the concept it is thought the readers will already have

2.5   **What criticism would you make of the statements below? How would you modify them?**
1. *Globalization is the intensification of economic, political, social and cultural relations across borders.*
2. *Developing countries are those countries which were previously colonized.*
3. *Subsistence farming is when rural communities have grown their own food.*

Formal definitions

The definitions given in Ex 2.5 are known as *formal definitions*. They follow a particular pattern of sentence structure.

1		2		3
name of the term being defined	+ verb	class to which it belongs	+ who/which/ that/where	special features

If you use an expression like *may be defined as* or *can be defined as* instead of the verb *to be*, you are being more 'honest' in accepting that there might be alternative definitions.

Example:

Travel may be defined as the <u>movement from one place to another</u>, often for a particular purpose.

2.6   **Write a formal definition for the words 1–3.**

1. university

2. research

3. library

Naming definitions

The three elements that make up a formal definition can be put in a different order to give a *naming definition*.

1		2		3
class to which it belongs	+ who/which/ that/where	special features	+ verb	name of the term being defined

Example:

The movement from one place to another, often for a particular purpose, may be defined as <u>travel</u>.

2.7   **In Ex 2.6 you wrote three formal definitions. Now write three naming definitions for the same words.**

2.8   **Study these four definitions and decide whether they are formal or naming definitions. Write *F* (formal) or *N* (naming).**

1. The period after independence is sometimes called neo-colonialism – the continuation of colonial exploitation without formal political control. This concept also covers the relationship of the Third World with the United States, which (with a few exceptions) was not a formal colonizer in the first place. And it covers the North–South international relations of Latin American states that have been independent for almost two centuries. _____

2. Biodiversity is the tremendous diversity of plant and animal species making up the Earth's (global, regional and local) ecosystems. _____

3. The massive transfer of agricultural technology coordinated through international agencies is called the Green Revolution. _____

4. Refugees are people fleeing to find refuge from war, natural disaster or political persecution. _____

Source: Adapted from Goldstein, J. S. (1996). *International relations*. New York: HarperCollins (pp. 434, 484, 496, 531).

2.9 **Find a definition in Text 6b in the *Reading & Writing Source Book*. Is it a formal or a naming definition?**

2.10 **Choose four of the words in Ex 2.3 and write a definition for each, two formal and two naming definitions.**

Key writing skills: Formal and naming definitions

The choice of whether to use a formal or naming definition depends on the information you wish to emphasize (see the underlined phrases in the examples on page 52). Formal definitions begin with what is being defined and naming definitions begin with the definition itself.

> **Study tip**
>
> Adding definitions to your essay is another way of making it appear more authoritative, as well as helping you clarify your own ideas. Using both formal and naming definitions is a way of introducing variety into your essays.

| Task 3 | **Microskills: Writing extended definitions** |

3.1 **Think of two different ways in which a definition could be extended. Discuss your ideas with the class.**

3.2 **Study the following two extracts. How have the definitions been extended in these cases?**

1. Technological transfer refers to a Third-World state's acquisition of technology (knowledge, skills, methods, designs, specialized equipment, and so on) from foreign sources, usually in conjunction with direct foreign investment or similar business operations. For example, a Third-World state may allow an MNC (a multinational corporation) to produce certain goods in the country under favorable conditions, provided the MNC shares knowledge of the technology and design behind the product. The state may try to get its own citizens into the management and professional workforce of factories or facilities created by foreign investment. In this way, not only does physical capital accumulate in the country, so does the related technological base for further development. However, MNCs are sometimes reluctant to share proprietary technology.

2. In the field of international relations, governmental loans are funds given to help in economic development, which must be repaid in the future out of the surplus generated by the development process ... unlike commercial loans, government-to-government development loans are often on subsidized terms, with long repayment times and low interest rates. Although still an obligation for the recipient country, such loans are relatively easy to service and thus do not hold back the country's accumulation of surplus in the short term.

Source: ibid., p. 541.

3.3   **Read these definitions and answer the questions.**
1. What is being defined in each case?
2. Why do you think the subjects are defined as a branch of a wider subject?

1. Anthropology may be defined as a branch of both science and sociology in which people, society and culture are studied.

2. Physics may be defined as a branch of science in which forces such as heat, light, sound, pressure, gravity and electricity, and the way that they affect objects, are studied.

Note: You will sometimes find yourself in an academic environment with students who are going to study different subjects to yours. In this case, you may want to explain your subject to them.

3.4   **Study the following definition of *psychology*. How has it been extended and how do you expect the writer to continue?**

1. Psychology may be defined as the science that studies the behaviour of man and other animals. For this definition to be useful, it is necessary to specify more clearly what psychologists mean by behaviour. An idea of the meaning of behaviour can be gained if the topics covered by psychology are examined: the behaving organism, growth and development, motivation and emotion, perception, learning and thinking, individuality and personality, conflict, adjustment and mental health, and social aspects of psychology. The behaving organism is important because, as a science rooted in biology, psychology is interested in the bodily processes that make activity possible …

Source: Buzan, T. (1971). *Speed reading*. Newton Abbot: David and Charles.

3.5   **Write an <u>extended definition</u> of your subject. Compare with another student and discuss any difficulties you had.**

> **Study tip**
>
> Writing extended definitions will help you think more carefully about your intended audience and what they need to know.

_____

_____

_____

_____

_____

_____

_____

_____

_____

3.6   Read the extract from Text 6b. Then answer questions 1–6.

Definitions of international HRM

There is no consensus about what the term 'IHRM' covers, although most studies in the area have traditionally focused on the area of expatriation (Brewster & Harris, 1999). IHRM has been defined as 'the HRM issues and problems arising from the internationalization of business, and the HRM strategies, policies and practices which firms pursue in response to the internationalization of business' (Scullion, 1995). Welch (1994) concluded that international HRM was essentially concerned with the four core activities of recruitment and selection, training and development, compensation, and the repatriation of expatriates. Iles (1995) agrees with regard to the first two activities but replaces the latter two with the management of multicultural teams, and international diversity and performance management. An alternative view is argued by Hendry (1994), who sees the three main issues as firstly, the management and development of expatriates; secondly, the internationalization of management throughout the organization; and finally, the need to internationalize the whole organization by creating a new corporate culture that addresses the need for greater international experience, given the increasing frequency of cross-cultural interactions while doing business at home as well as abroad. Such definitions highlight IHRM as a field related to, but separate from, comparative employment relations, which is concerned with understanding in what ways and why HRM practices differ across countries (Bamber & Lansbury, 1998).

1. How many definitions are in the paragraph?
2. What language do the writers use to introduce each definition?
3. Why do the writers include the definition of IHRM?
4. Why do the writers introduce an 'alternative' view?
5. What information is in the paragraph leader?
6. What information is in the concluding sentence?

3.7   Read a second extract from Text 6b and answer these questions.
1. What is the main focus of the paragraph?
2. How do the writers develop their discussion of the definitions of HRM?

More recent definitions emphasize a more strategic approach and consider the role and organization of IHRM functions and the relationship between headquarters and local units, as well as the actual policies and practices adopted. They tend to focus on how multinational corporations manage their geographically dispersed workforces in order to leverage (i.e., make best use of) their HR resources for both local and global competitive advantage (Schuler et al., 2002). Globalization has brought new challenges and increased complexity, including the challenge of managing newer forms of network organization. In recognition of such developments, some experts have developed new definitions where IHRM is seen as playing a key role in achieving a balance between the need for control and coordination of foreign subsidiaries, and the need to adapt to local environments. More recently, definitions have been extended to cover localization of management, international coordination, global leadership development and the emerging cultural challenges of global knowledge management (Evans et al., 2002). This suggests that developing future global leaders is a key priority in the management of human resources in the global firm (Gregerson et al., 1998; Scullion & Starkey, 2000).

3.8 **Decide on content from the source material that you will use in your essay.**

  a. Discuss with another student how you will use information from these extracts in your own essay.

  b. Think about what definitions would be useful in your essay on human resource management. Write the definitions below.

_____

_____

_____

_____

_____

Task 4	**Microskills: Paragraph development – exemplification and support**

In academic writing, it is important to support your ideas with examples and details; this involves making use of **critical reading** and **critical thinking** skills. In this task, and in Unit 7, you will look at ways of doing this.

4.1 **What different methods can you use to support and develop your ideas in an essay? Discuss your ideas with another student.**

4.2 **Read the following extract and think about how the writer supports his ideas. Questions 1–3 will guide your evaluation.**

  1. What is the main idea being discussed in the paragraph?

  2. How have the writers supported the main idea of the paragraph?

  3. How has this information helped you, the reader, understand more about the main idea?

1. **a** In the last 20 years, a series of technological and political changes have transformed the televisual landscape and have contributed to the globalization of television as a medium and as an industry. **b** First and foremost, the number of countries with broadcasting systems and the number of televisions available on which to watch their output has steadily risen. **c** From its Western core, television has spread in the post-war years across Eastern Europe and the Soviet Union, into Latin America, Asia and Africa. **d** Second, first within the West, but later in other areas as well, the number of terrestrial channels has steadily climbed. **e** In part, this has been because governments have been prepared to enlarge the funding base for television companies, for there is clearly a limit to the number of channels and programmes that can be funded by subsidy/licence fee alone. **f** By allowing advertising revenue and sponsorship into the television funding mix – be it through public corporations taking advertising or wholly private stations – the potential output and funding base of national television has risen. **g** However, the expansion of output has rarely, if ever, been matched by a corresponding increase in the capacity of national audiovisual industries to supply all of the potential broadcast slots. **h** Thus, the expansion of television output across and within countries has fuelled the demand for television imports.

Source: Held, et al. (1999).

Discuss your ideas with your partner.

In the text in Ex 4.2, the writer has stated the main idea within the paragraph leader, '… *technological and political changes have transformed the televisual landscape* …'. The writer continues by explaining the impact in more detail. The writer helps the reader follow the supporting arguments by using markers: *First and foremost* (sentence b); *Second* (sentence d). This is an important element you should include in your own writing.

One way of ensuring that you, as the writer, explain your points in detail to your reader, is to check any questions that can be asked about the main idea(s) in your statement of the topic.

4.3   **You can identify necessary supporting detail by asking yourself questions about the paragraph leader.**

One question you can ask about the ideas in the paragraph leader is:

What technological and political changes have occurred in the last 20 years?

Write down other questions you could ask.

_____

_____

_____

4.4   **Using the extract from Held et al. (1999) from Ex 4.2, find the answers to questions 1–4. Write the letter(s) identifying the sentences which answer the questions.**

1. What technological and political changes have occurred in the last 20 years?

_____

2. How have these technological and political changes transformed the televisual landscape?

_____

3. How have these technological and political changes contributed to the globalization of television as a medium?

_____

4. How have these technological and political changes contributed to the globalization of television as an industry?

_____

You will see that sentence b is part of the answer to question 2, as it explains that the number of countries with access to television has risen. A question the reader might then ask is *Which countries?* Sentence c answers this question.

This shows that the writers have anticipated questions a reader might ask about a statement they have made. By explaining their ideas adequately, they have presented a text that flows logically and coherently.

4.5   **Use the text in Ex 4.2 to answer these questions.**

   1. What is the function of sentence g?

_____

   2. What is the function of sentence h?

_____

4.6 **Read the paragraph below from Text 5b and answer questions 1–4. The sentences in the text are marked a–g to make it easier to answer.**

1. What is the topic of the paragraph, as indicated in the paragraph leader?
2. What questions can you ask about the idea(s) in the paragraph leader?
3. Does the writer answer these questions?
4. What is the purpose of:
   a. sentence e?
   b. sentence f?
   c. sentence g?

a Patterns in global food prices are indicators of how the availability of food changes, at least for those who can afford it and have access to world markets. **b** Over the past century, gross food prices have generally fallen, levelling off in the past three decades but punctuated by price spikes such as that caused by the 1970s oil crisis. **c** In mid-2008, there was an unexpected rapid rise in food prices – the cause of which is still being debated – that subsided when the world economy went into recession (Piesse & Thirtle, 2009). **d** However, many (but not all) commentators have predicted that this spike heralds a period of rising and more volatile food prices driven primarily by increased demand from rapidly developing countries, as well as by competition for resources from first-generation biofuels production (Royal Society, 2008). **e** Increased food prices will stimulate greater investment in food production, but the critical importance of food to human well-being and also to social and political stability makes it likely that governments and other organizations will want to encourage food production beyond that driven by simple market mechanisms (Skidelsky, 2009). **f** However, there are serious concerns about changes in food production patterns where production of traditional staple food sources is flattening out rather than rising in line with the population explosion (Figure 1). **g** The long-term nature of returns on investment for many aspects of food production and the importance of policies that promote sustainability and equal treatment for all also argue against relying purely on market solutions.

4.7 **Read the paragraph below from Text 2a and answer questions 1–4. The sentences in the text are marked a–h to make it easier to answer.**

1. What is the topic of the paragraph, as indicated in the paragraph leader?
2. What questions can you ask about the idea(s) in the paragraph leader?
3. Does the writer answer these questions?
4. What is the purpose of:
   a. sentences d and f?
   b. sentence h?

a In the United States, biogas systems are quite rare. **b** There are currently only 151 biomass digesters in the country, most of them small and using only manure, according to the Environmental Protection Agency. **c** The EPA has estimated that installing such plants would actually be feasible at about 8,000 US farms. **d** However, so far, such projects have been limited by high initial costs, scant government financing and the lack of a business model. **e** There is no supply network for moving manure to a centralized plant and no outlet to sell the biogas generated. **f** Still, a number of states and companies are considering new investment. **g** Two California utilities, Southern California Gas and San Diego Gas & Electric, have filed for permission with the state's Public Utilities Commission to build plants in California to turn organic waste from farms and gas from water treatment plants into biogas that would feed into the state's natural-gas pipelines after purification. **h** Using biogas would help the utilities meet requirements in California and many other states to generate a portion of their power using renewable energy within the coming decade.

Key writing skills: Thinking critically

To ensure that you support your main ideas with adequate explanation for your reader, ask questions about the ideas in your paragraph leader (*What? Why? How? Who? When?*), and then answer them. You should also give examples, comment on the ideas you discuss, and then write a concluding sentence.

As a writer, it is important to 'round up' any discussion of your ideas with a comment and a conclusion (in a concluding sentence). This shows that you are thinking critically about your ideas.

Task 5	**Using examples to develop your ideas**

In Text 2a, from Ex 4.7, the information in sentence g answers the question *Which companies are considering new investment?* This sentence develops the writer's ideas further, by providing a specific example.

In your writing, you can use certain expressions to indicate to the reader that you are introducing an example. These expressions will help the reader to follow what is being discussed.

5.1   **Write some expressions that can introduce an example into your writing.**

_____

_____

_____

5.2   **Compare your expressions with ones that your teacher will give you.**

1. How many are the same?
2. How many did you use appropriately?

5.3   **Complete each of the following texts using one of the expressions supplied by your teacher. Do not use any expression more than once.**

Note: There is one expression that you will *not* use.

1. There are three main aspects which influence academic success; these can be classified as: learning environment, social pressure and competition, and personal growth. First of all, schools should offer good learning environments, such as a good library, qualified teachers, and the latest equipment. Secondly, students may receive support or pressure from their parents, or encounter competition among their peers. _____, they need their parents' financial support in order to complete their academic studies. Families might pressure their children to study to an advanced level because they feel this will bring them more success in the future. Finally, by working to achieve personal growth, students can increase their chance of academic success. _____, they can learn how to communicate with other people, how to cooperate with classmates and how to be a leader in a group discussion or a case study. Personal growth can also be achieved by joining a club, talking with a tutor, doing a project or a dissertation, or participating in group discussions.

2. Nurture strongly influences human development. _____ is the example of a newborn baby, lost in the forest. An old and kind wolf finds him, takes him in and feeds him with her own milk. She uses wolf language to communicate with him. After a few months the baby thrives; this baby has human genes and features, but lives in a wolf environment, and behaves accordingly. As he has been so strongly influenced by this environment, perhaps he would just as easily re-adapt to human society after a period of time.

3. Many people agree that babies develop as a result of the environment in which they live. _____ is that children, reared in an environment in which people talk to them and reward them for making speechlike sounds, talk earlier than children who do not receive the same experience. Similarly, a study by Zelazo et al. (1972) indicated that if parents help an infant to step forwards for a few minutes several times a day in the first two months, he/she will begin walking five to seven weeks earlier than other infants who have not had this practice.

4. However, sometimes the fax machine and e-mail are used in a negative way, _____ the delivery of junk and abusive mail, as it is difficult to discover the identity of the sender.

5. One advantage of having an open market is the fact that new companies can enter the market, so the customer can have a wider choice of product. There will also be more competition between the companies to create the best product, thus eliminating low-quality products from the market. _____ is the growing market for mobile phones in Colombia. Two companies are trying to enter the market by offering free mobile phones.

Sources: Edited extracts from authentic student material.

| Task 6 | **Writing your essay** |

6.1 **Look at the plan for your essay. Where could you improve your essay by incorporating definitions and support for your ideas?**

Write the first draft of your essay.

6.2 **Read and evaluate the first draft of another student's essay.**
When you finish your first draft, exchange drafts with another student. Read your partner's draft carefully and respond to the questions on the peer evaluation sheet for Unit 6 (see page 89).

Unit summary

In this unit you have practised writing definitions. You have also focused on how to develop your ideas by using background support and examples.

1 **How could you explain the following to another student?**

a. a formal definition

b. a naming definition

c. an extended definition

2 **Identify the function of the highlighted sections in each extract below.**

a. In the last ten years, the landscape has been transformed. Firstly, the number of households using the technology has increased …

b. Recently there has been substantial population growth. There have been several surveys which indicate …

c. The open market has certain disadvantages. A case in point is …

d. Expenditure on leisure increases during the summer. This is due to increased tourism.

3 **Complete this summary using your own words.**

This unit has helped me develop my ideas in an essay more effectively by _____

_____

_____

_____

_____

_____

_____

For web resources relevant to this book, see:
www.englishforacademicstudy.com
These weblinks will provide you with help in writing definitions as well as links to articles about human resource management.

Sustainable fashion

In this unit you will:

- analyze essay titles and decide on appropriate organizational patterns
- consider the development of cause-and-effect relationships in your writing
- include statistics to support your ideas

Texts	Sustainable fashion, Texts 7a–7c (Source Book pp. 45–54)

In this unit you will read three extracts from various sources on sustainable fashion (Texts 7a–7c in the *Reading & Writing Source Book*). This will prepare you to write the following essay:

 The fashion industry poses a serious threat to the environment. A higher level of sustainability in materials production is the key solution. Discuss.

Task 1	**Analyzing the question**

You have worked on analyzing the essay question in Unit 6. You will follow the same procedure for the essay title above.

1.1 **Read the essay title above and answer these questions.**
   1. How many parts to the title are there?
   2. What are the key ideas in the essay title?

   Discuss your ideas with another student.

1.2 **What do you think is the best way to organize your ideas for this title?**

   Discuss your ideas with another student.

1.3 **Write down any ideas you think might be relevant to the essay topic in five minutes.**

   Use notes and write them in the order you think of them.

Task 2	**Microskills: Organizing your essay – cause and effect**

In Unit 5, you looked at organizing your essays using the SPSIE pattern. You may have decided in Ex 1.1 that this pattern is appropriate for the essay about the fashion industry, because the word *solution* is one of the key words in the essay title.

However, you may have decided that there are *two* parts to the writing task. In the first part, you might want to explain why the fashion industry poses a serious threat to the environment, i.e., explain the *causes* of the situation. In the second part, you might want to explain how the problem could be solved, and whether producing more sustainable materials is a key solution.

2.1 **If you think about the organization of your essay as two parts which require different patterns, how could you organize your ideas:**
1. in the first part?
2. in the second part?

2.2 **Read the following student essay entitled** *Discuss the positive and negative effects of tourism on people and the environment.* **Identify the purpose of each paragraph.**
Make notes in the spaces provided below and highlight key points that help you decide. Ignore the underlined expressions at this stage.

(1) Since the end of the Second World War, the developed countries have made very significant leaps in progress. <u>A consequence of</u> this development for the populations of these countries has been that their standards of living have risen year after year. They have now reached a situation in which most of the people are living a healthy and comfortable life. Parallel to the rise in standards of living, many people have developed a strong desire to visit different parts of the world, resulting in a steep rise in foreign tourism. Nowadays, it is common for people to take a holiday in a foreign country rather than in their own native country. This essay will attempt to discuss the effects of tourism on people and the environment.

_____

_____

(2) Most people tend to take a holiday at least once a year; for some people it is almost a duty. <u>Owing to</u> the rising standards of living, people, especially from the developed countries, do not hesitate to spend large amounts of money on the pleasure of having a break far from their permanent residence. Travel agencies and tourism companies have capitalized on this trend; they display advertisements with attractive pictures, and offer affordable prices with the aim of enticing more people to travel the world on holiday. <u>This has caused</u> the number of people who travel for their holidays to multiply many times over the last few decades. As holidaymakers tend to travel to tropical areas and coastal towns where they can enjoy permanent sunshine, beaches or extensive forest areas, it seems that no part of the world has been untouched by tourism.

_____

_____

(3) The millions of holidaymakers who travel the world looking for new places have caused serious problems for the local population and for the environment of the destination countries. In fact, one result of the rising numbers of tourists visiting developing countries is that a certain proportion of the local population has developed illegal activities. For instance, the trade in ivory products has increased at the expense of elephants, especially in the Ivory Coast and Kenya. Another example is the trade in Siberian tiger furs which is threatening the species with extinction. Worse still, particularly in South Asia, the population has suffered from the rapid proliferation of prostitution, mainly due to the large number of people reportedly practising sex tourism. Thailand, where minors are occasionally sold by their parents, is a case in point.

_____

_____

(4) Another harmful effect of tourism is the damage it causes to the environment. In fact, as a result of the large number of tourists visiting some parts of the world, environmental damage has reached serious proportions and natural resources have been degraded. An example of this is the Mediterranean Sea, which is reported to be the dirtiest sea in the world because of sewage contamination; German coasts have also been polluted by effluent from the many cruising boats; in France, where sewage is sometimes discharged directly into streams, most of those in the Pyrenees are now polluted. Above all, the dense aerial traffic created by the active movement of holidaymakers has caused an alarming rise in air pollution; this gives rise to acid rain that, in turn, contaminates soils and causes serious damage to forest areas. For example, 60% of the Alpine forests in France are reported to be experiencing serious degradation. So it would seem that mass tourism has resulted in very serious problems for both the people and the environment of the destination countries.

(5) The rising intensity of the threat that mass tourism represents has prompted some governments and non-governmental organizations to act swiftly. In fact, some governments have made considerable efforts to sensitize their populations to the threat that tourism represents to the environment; campaigns have been launched and money has been spent to protect the environment and to counteract the environmental damage that has already occurred. In France, for example, the government spends billions of euros on ways to protect the national nature reserves from tourist-related waste and tidy the beaches and mountain villages. It is also engaged in creating tree plantations to replace trees destroyed by acid rain. In York, in England, many residents wear anti-tourist badges in protest against the increase in the number of tourists. Access to many monuments, such as the Leaning Tower of Pisa in Italy and the Parthenon in Athens, is extremely restricted. In addition, local governments in Africa, with the help of non-governmental organizations like Greenpeace, have declared war on the illegal trade in ivory and the fur from wild animals that are currently menaced with extinction. It therefore seems that significant effort has been made in different parts of the world where nature appears to be threatened.

(6) The solutions that have been adopted by governments have not shown much effectiveness or efficiency, however. Although governments have made serious efforts to deal with the problems, sometimes by enacting strict new laws, mass tourism is still causing many problems, and the intensity of degradation that has been registered in the environment has not declined. Also, the traffic in ivory and rare animal furs has considerably increased, and gangs are becoming more organized because of the potential profits that can be obtained from this traffic. The strict laws do not seem to dissuade the gangs from carrying out these illegal and destructive activities. In addition, in spite of the huge efforts made by the international courts and the organizations for the protection and promotion of children's rights, there are still hundreds of thousands of tourists who are reported to practise sex tourism and to abuse poverty.

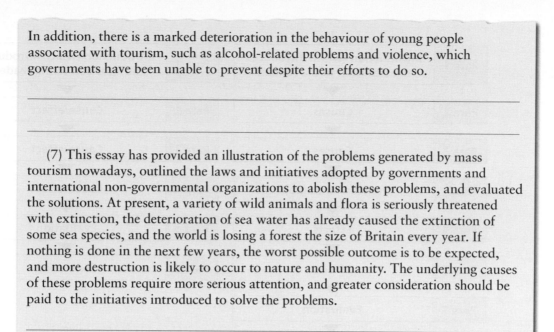

In addition, there is a marked deterioration in the behaviour of young people associated with tourism, such as alcohol-related problems and violence, which governments have been unable to prevent despite their efforts to do so.

(7) This essay has provided an illustration of the problems generated by mass tourism nowadays, outlined the laws and initiatives adopted by governments and international non-governmental organizations to abolish these problems, and evaluated the solutions. At present, a variety of wild animals and flora is seriously threatened with extinction, the deterioration of sea water has already caused the extinction of some sea species, and the world is losing a forest the size of Britain every year. If nothing is done in the next few years, the worst possible outcome is to be expected, and more destruction is likely to occur to nature and humanity. The underlying causes of these problems require more serious attention, and greater consideration should be paid to the initiatives introduced to solve the problems.

Source: Edited extracts from authentic student material.

2.3 **Look back at the essay title in Ex 2.2. Decide whether the writer has addressed all parts of the question in the essay. For example:**
1. Are all the paragraphs necessary?
2. Are all the relevant points appropriately developed?
3. What other questions can you ask to evaluate the success of this essay?

2.4 **Study the two simple models on page 68. Then think about them in relation to the essay you have just read. Use these questions to help you.**
1. Which of the two models is most similar to the essay structure?
2. What are the advantages and disadvantages of each model?

Note: There are a number of different ways of developing an essay that involves an explanation and analysis of the causes and effects of a situation.

Discuss your answers with another student.

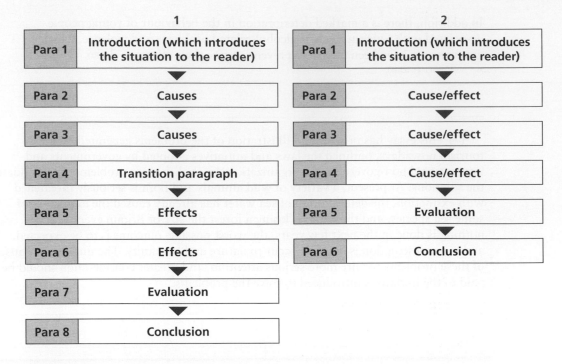

	1			**2**	
Para 1	Introduction (which introduces the situation to the reader)		Para 1	Introduction (which introduces the situation to the reader)	
Para 2	Causes		Para 2	Cause/effect	
Para 3	Causes		Para 3	Cause/effect	
Para 4	Transition paragraph		Para 4	Cause/effect	
Para 5	Effects		Para 5	Evaluation	
Para 6	Effects		Para 6	Conclusion	
Para 7	Evaluation				
Para 8	Conclusion				

2.5 **Study the underlined expressions in the student essay in Ex 2.2 and answer the questions.**

1. What function do these expressions have within or between the sentences?

2. Note down any similar expressions you can find in paragraphs 3–6.

3. Note down more expressions you know with the same function.

Compare your answers with your partner.

Key writing skills: Using multiple organization structures in your writing

Academic writing often requires a discussion of the causes and effects of a situation or problem. This is a common approach to problem-solving in academic life. Such a discussion would be appropriate for the first part of your essay on sustainable fashion.

This means that you need to make use of:

- appropriate patterns of organization
- appropriate patterns of language

By doing so, you will make the link between cause and effect clear and explicit.

2.6 **Write sentences to connect the ideas. The first two are given as examples.**

Use some of the expressions discussed in Ex 2.5.

1. air travel–airports

Since there is such a demand for air travel, the government is building more airports.

2. infected mosquitoes–malaria

Due to the rising number of infected mosquitoes, malaria has become an even worse threat to health than in the 1990s.

3. rain–floods

4. globalization–cultural covergence

5. fear–adrenalin

6. inflation–unemployment

7. arid climate–irrigate fields

8. absenteeism–low productivity

9. lack of plants–soil erosion

10. satellites–mobile phone

11. high birth rate–overcrowding

Useful expressions to express cause and effect

a. Using *cause* as a noun

The | direct / likely / major / main | cause of death was a serious bacterial infection.

The cause of the damage was not known.

Structure: the + (adjective) + cause + of + noun + verb to be + noun phrase/verb phrase

b. Using *reason* as a noun

The | main / first/second/third | reason for choosing a university is its academic reputation.

One | key | reason for entering higher education is to improve employment prospects.

Structure: the + (adjective) + reason + for + _____ ing + noun + verb to be + noun phrase/verb phrase

The main reason for inflation is the rising cost of oil.

Structure: the + (adjective) + reason + for + noun + verb to be + noun phrase/verb phrase

c. Using *cause* as a verb

Student loans | may / can / will | cause financial problems for some categories of graduates.

Falls in the Asian stock market may cause significant damage to markets in the United States and Europe.

Structure: noun + (modal auxiliary verb) + cause + noun phrase

d. Using *result* as a verb

The rise in house prices | may / can / will | result in fewer young people buying their first home.

Structure: noun phrase + (modal auxiliary verb) result + in + noun phrase

e. Using *effect* (noun) pattern 1

The effect of loan sales is an immediate improvement in the public finances.

The effect of greenhouse gases is to warm the atmosphere.

Structure: the + (adjective) + effect of noun + verb to be + noun phrase/verb phrase

f. Using *effect* (noun) pattern 2

Violence on television can have a(n) | substantial / adverse / strong | effect on the behaviour of children.

Loans may have a disincentive effect on the willingness of individuals from low socioeconomic groups to participate in higher education.

Structure: noun + (modal auxiliary verb) + have + a/an + (adjective) + effect + on + noun phrase

g. Using *affect* (verb)

The increase in greenhouse gases in the atmosphere significantly affects some of the continental-scale patterns of climate change.

Adverse weather conditions can affect the psychological state of human beings.

Structure: noun + | adverb / modal auxiliary verb | + affect(s) + noun phrase

h. Using the first conditional

When there is a dense accumulation of pollutants in the air, people often become ill.

When a reduction in the available research funds occurs, there is a decrease in the number of medical research projects.

Structure: When + cause + effect

Task 3 Writing your essay

Task 2 looked at ways of developing cause-and-effect relationships in your writing. It is important to remember that a response to an essay task will usually involve more than one pattern of organization, as already discussed.

3.1 **Discuss with a partner how you can organize your ideas.**

3.2 **Read Texts 7a–7c and decide what information you can use in your essay. Review the notes and organization you worked on in Task 1.**

3.3 **Write your essay plan.**

3.4 **Read the essay plan of another student. Provide constructive feedback on the following points:**
- relevance of response to the task
- logic of order of ideas
- effectiveness of examples
- clarity of thesis

Write the first draft of your essay.

3.5 **Read and evaluate the first draft of another student's essay.**
When you finish your first draft, exchange your draft with another student. Read your partner's draft carefully and respond to the questions on the peer evaluation sheet for Unit 7 (see page 90).

Task 4 Microskills: Using statistical facts

Another way of supporting your argument is by using statistical facts.

4.1 **Think about the different ways statistics can be displayed. Why are different methods of display used?**
Discuss your ideas with another student.

4.2 **Study Table 1 and answer these questions.**
1. What information is particularly interesting?
2. What reasons can you think of to explain any information in the table?

Table 1: Readership of national daily newspapers, 1971–2010

Great Britain	Percentages				
	1971	1981	1991	2001	2010
Sun	17	26	22	20	16
Daily Mail	12	12	10	12	10
Daily Mirror	34	25	22	12	7

Daily Telegraph	9	8	6	5	4
Times	3	2	2	3	3
Daily Express	24	14	8	4	3
Daily Star	-	9	6	3	3
Guardian	3	3	3	2	2
Independent	-	-	2	1	1
Financial Times	2	2	2	1	1
Any national daily newspaper	-	72	62	53	41

Source: Text and tables adapted from Seddon, C. (2011). Lifestyles and social participation. In Beaumont, J. (Ed.). *Social Trends 41* (Newport: Office for National Statistics). Retrieved May 17, 2011, from www.statistics.gov.uk.

4.3   **Read the commentary below on Table 1 from Ex 4.2. Answer the following questions. The sentences have been numbered to help you.**

1. What is the main purpose of the commentary?
2. What are the main points of interest highlighted by the writer?

(1) The estimated proportion of adults aged 15 and over in Great Britain who read a national daily newspaper has been decreasing over the past 30 years, from 72 per cent of adults in 1981 to 41 per cent in 2010, according to the National Readership Survey (Table 1). (2) On average, since 1981 the proportion reading national newspapers has fallen by approximately ten percentage points every ten years.

(3) The most commonly read newspaper in 2010 was the *Sun*, though readership has decreased from 26 per cent of adults who read newspapers in 1981 to 16 per cent in 2010. (4) In fact, most tabloid newspapers experienced substantial falls in readership over this period. (5) The *Daily Mirror* suffered the largest decrease, falling from being the most commonly read in 1971, when 34 per cent of adults read it, to 7 per cent in 2010. (6) The *Daily Express* has also suffered a similar fate, falling from 24 per cent in 1971 to 3 per cent in 2010.

(7) The readership of most other newspapers has remained stable, fluctuating by only one or two percentage points over the period. (8) These are mainly the broadsheets, which have kept their smaller but more targeted audiences.

(9) The decline in the proportion of those reading national newspapers may be affected by the availability of news websites which are free on the Internet. (10) A recent survey by YouGov asked whether respondents would consider paying for access to online news sites. (11) Only 2 per cent stated yes they definitely would, while a further 4 per cent said they would pay but only for special content, for instance content not available elsewhere. (12) A further 6 per cent stated they might possibly pay for online content, while the majority (83 per cent) stated that they would not consider paying for access to newspapers online (YouGov, 2010b).

Source: ibid

4.4 **Analyze the use of tenses in the commentary.**
a. Underline the main verbs in each sentence.
b. Complete the table with the tense and the reason for its use.

Sentence	Verb(s)	Tense	Reason
1	has been decreasing	present perfect continuous	describes an ongoing trend
2			
3			
4			
5			
6			
7			
8			
9			
10			
11			
12			

4.5 **Discuss your answers in groups of three and then with the rest of the class.**

4.6 **Use the statistics in Table 2 to write a paragraph that develops the following topic sentence.**

There are certain noticeable differences in free-time activities between older and younger people in the UK.

Table 2: Selected activities performed in free time[1] by age, 2009/2010*

	16–24	25–34	35–44	45–64	65 and over	All aged 16 and over
Watching television	88	85	88	89	92	89
Spending time with friends/family	87	85	85	83	82	84
Listening to music	90	78	76	74	69	76
Shopping	71	73	74	69	69	71
Reading	53	62	65	72	73	67
Eating out at restaurants	66	71	70	72	73	67
Days out	54	65	68	67	59	63
Internet/e-mailing	79	77	71	57	24	59
Sport/exercise	63	63	60	55	35	54
Gardening	16	36	51	64	62	49
Going to pubs/bars/clubs	59	63	50	44	33	48
Going to the cinema	72	61	55	42	21	48

[1]**Respondents were shown a list of activities and asked to pick the things they did in their free time in the last year prior to interview. The most popular activities performed by all adults aged 16 and over are shown in the table.**

Source: ibid.

*Figures given as percentages

4.7 **Think about how you could use the following bar chart in your essay for this unit.**

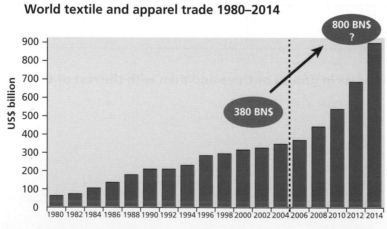

World textile and apparel trade 1980–2014

Source: Textile Exchange (2011). *Industry overview.* Retrieved May 17, 2011, from www.teonline/industry-overview.html

Make appropriate changes to your essay for Unit 7, considering the work you have carried out in Tasks 3 and 4.

Unit summary

In this unit you have looked at different ways of organizing the contents of an essay. You have also worked on incorporating ideas from your reading into your essay.

1 **Think about and/or discuss your answers to the following questions.**

a.
> I have trouble knowing when to start a new paragraph when I write essays. Will it help if I use the same basic paragraph organization for all my essays?

b.
> My essay is supposed to be on the advantages and disadvantages of tourism in developing countries, but I can't think of many disadvantages. How important is it to look at negative effects as well as positive ones?

c.
> How flexible should the plan for my essay be? For example, do I have to have three paragraphs on the advantages of a situation, and three paragraphs on the disadvantages?

d.
> Why is it important to use particular language patterns in different types of essays? For example, in a cause-and-effect essay, do I need to use the language expressions on pages 69–70? Should I vary the expressions I use? I get confused about the different grammar patterns.

2 **Choose the best option to complete the sentences below.**

a. The decision on how to organize your essay should depend on *the topic of the essay / your tutor's preference*.

b. You need to plan your paragraphs and edit them after you have written your first draft so that each paragraph has a clear *ending / function*.

c. It is important to answer the essay question fully and give a balanced answer. For example, if you are asked to discuss advantages and disadvantages, you *should try to / don't need to* give equal attention to both sides of the argument.

d. You can use different patterns to organize your essays. As you become more skilled and confident, you can *be more flexible / write longer paragraphs*.

e. If you are aware of, and able to use, common essay-writing expressions, it will make the ideas in your essay *less exciting and original / clearer and easier to follow*.

For web resources relevant to this book, see:
www.englishforacademicstudy.com
This weblink will provide you with help in organizing your essay by expressing cause and effect, using statistics to support your ideas and a useful article explaining sustainable fashion.

8 The Tipping Point

In this unit you will:

- analyze essay titles and decide on appropriate organizational patterns
- consider the development of compare-and-contrast relationships in your writing
- incorporate ideas from sources as quotations to support your ideas

Texts | The Tipping Point, Texts 8a–8e (Source Book pp. 55–68)

You will read five extracts from various sources related to the author Malcolm Gladwell and his book *The Tipping Point* in this unit (Texts 8a–8e in the *Reading & Writing Source Book*). This will prepare you to write the following essay:

> Compare and contrast the role of Innovators and Early Adopters with the role of the Early Majority in achieving commercial success. Relate your answer to Gladwell's theory of the Tipping Point.

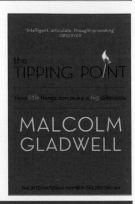

Task 1 | Background reading

1.1 **Read the first two texts for this unit, Texts 8a and 8b.**
These texts will help you develop the ideas for your essay.

Task 2 | Analyzing the question

2.1 **Follow the same procedure as in Units 6 and 7 to analyze the essay title.**
If you are not sure of the procedure, refer to Unit 6, Task 1.

2.2 **You have now analyzed the question. What do you think is the best way to organize your ideas for this essay? Discuss your ideas with another student.**

2.3 **In five minutes, make notes on any ideas you have that are relevant to this essay.**

2.4 **How can you relate your discussion to theory?**

Task 3	**Microskills: Organizing your essay – comparison and contrast**

A description based on comparison and contrast can be developed in two ways. For the purposes of clarity, the ideas and information being compared and contrasted in Figures 1 and 2 have been called Information A and Information B.

a. **Vertical pattern:** You can *group* the main ideas about Information A in one paragraph or section and the main ideas about Information B in the next paragraph or section. This can be described as a 'vertical' pattern, as represented in Figure 1.

Figure 1

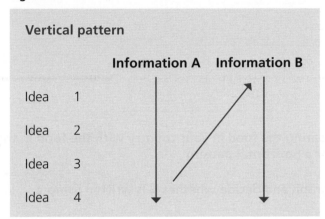

b. **Horizontal pattern:** Alternatively, you can treat the corresponding ideas in Information A and Information B as a *pair* and compare and contrast them *one after the other*. This can be described as a 'horizontal' pattern, as represented in Figure 2.

Figure 2

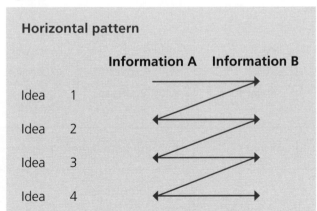

Whether you choose the vertical pattern or the horizontal pattern depends on three main factors:
- the kind of text you are writing
- the purpose of the text
- your own preference

Some writers and readers find the horizontal pattern clearer because it reminds them of the comparison-and-contrast relationship. Others prefer the vertical pattern because of its relative simplicity. The horizontal pattern can be more suitable for a longer piece of writing. Both patterns are commonly used in descriptions involving comparison and contrast.

3.1 **Study the paragraph below. Which pattern of organization does it follow?**

> Apples are generally oval in shape. They range in colour from green to yellow to red. Their texture is usually firm and sometimes even hard. Most oranges, however, are more round in shape. Their colour range is more limited – from vermilion to pale orange. In terms of texture they are relatively soft.

3.2 **Rewrite the paragraph so that it follows the opposite pattern of comparison and contrast.**

_____

_____

_____

_____

3.3 **Write a short paragraph comparing the food in your country with the food in the UK. Choose *either* a vertical *or* a horizontal pattern.**

3.4 **Read another student's paragraph and decide whether it is written using a vertical or horizontal pattern.**

3.5 **Rewrite your partner's paragraph using the opposite pattern.**

Key writing skills: Common expressions and markers for comparison and contrast

Comparison within sentences				
X is	very	like Y	in terms of	quality/size.
X and Y are	quite	similar	with respect to	expense.
X is	rather	similar to Y	with regard to	
X resembles Y		in that	they are both large/expensive.	
X is	exactly		the same as Y.	
	precisely			
	just			
	virtually			
	almost			
	nearly			
X is costly to buy		and	it is (also) costly to maintain.	

Comparison between sentences

X is expensive.	Similarly, Likewise, Moreover, Furthermore, In addition,	it is expensive to maintain/ operate.

Contrast within sentences

X is unlike Y X differs from Y X and Y differ X is different from Y X contrasts with Y	with respect to with regard to in terms of	size/expense, etc.
	in that X is smaller/more expensive, etc.	

X has four aspects,	whereas while but yet although	Y has three.

X is Y is	considerably a great deal (very) much rather a little slightly scarcely	smaller than Y. larger than X.

Contrast between sentences

X is expensive to buy.	However, Conversely, By/In contrast, On the other hand,	it is cheap to operate/maintain, etc.

3.6   **Think about how you can use some of these expressions into your essay. Discuss them with your partner.**

In Units 1 and 2, you completed a series of tasks to help you incorporate ideas from different sources into your writing. One of the aims of these tasks was to help you avoid plagiarizing the writing of others. Sometimes you can use the exact words of another writer to support your points; however, you should only use the original words in the following circumstances:

- when they are key to supporting your idea
- when you are using them to make an impact
- when you make it clear you are using another writer's words

4.1   **Read Text 8e, which is an extract from *The Tipping Point*. Decide which parts will be useful in your essay.**

Discuss your choices with another student.

4.2   **Look at the short extract below from Text 8e and answer questions 1–3.**
1. Do you feel this extract expresses a key point in the book?
2. Could you express the idea in a better way than in this extract?
3. How would you choose to incorporate it in your essay? By paraphrasing or directly quoting?

> Airwalk tipped because its advertising was founded very explicitly on the principles of epidemic transmission.

Key writing skills: Using direct quotations

You may wish to use the case of the success of *Airwalk* to illustrate a point you are making in relation to the Tipping Point theory. You may choose to use the above sentence as it is a key point and is very well expressed.

To avoid plagiarism with direct quotes, you need to introduce:
- the name of the author
- the year of publication
- the page number

This makes it clear that the idea(s) you have written are not your own. There are a number of ways of doing this; three of them are presented here:

> 1. As Gladwell (2010) emphasizes, 'Airwalk tipped because its advertising was founded very explicitly on the principles of epidemic transmission.' (p. 196)

> 2. Gladwell (2010) emphasizes that 'Airwalk tipped because its advertising was founded very explicitly on the principles of epidemic transmission.' (p. 196)

> 3. 'Airwalk tipped because its advertising was founded very explicitly on the principles of epidemic transmission.' (Gladwell, 2010, p. 196).

Answer the questions about these three ways of incorporating a quotation into academic writing.

1. Which sentence(s) use(s) a verb to introduce the quotation?

2. What difference(s) is/are there between the sentences using a verb?

3. What punctuation is used immediately before and after the original words?

4. What separates the year from the page number?

4.3 **Work with another student and brainstorm other verbs you can use to introduce quotations into your writing.**

4.4 **Use the three methods shown on page 80 to introduce the following quotation that appears in Text 8e.**

> … there is a substantial difference between the people who originate trends and ideas and the people in the Majority who eventually take them up.

4.5 **Study the following extract from a student's essay and answer the questions about the way it is written.**

> Gladwell (2010) summarizes Moore's argument as follows:
>
> … the attitude of the Early Adopters and the attitude of the Early Majority are fundamentally incompatible. Innovations don't just slide effortlessly from one group to the next. There is a chasm between them. All kinds of high-tech products fail, never making it beyond the Early Adopters, because the companies that make them can't find a way to transform an idea that makes perfect sense to an Early Adopter into one that makes perfect sense to a member of the Early Majority (pp. 198–199).

1. What are the differences compared with the quotation referred to in Ex 4.2?
2. How could you use this quotation in your essay? Why would you do this?

Key writing skills: Including extended quotations
You will usually include fairly short quotations in your essays. However, you may sometimes wish to use 40 or more words from the original text. In this case, you need to use different conventions. In APA style, the way to do this is to use a block quotation. Start the block quotation on a new line, and indent the block with five spaces (1.3cm).

4.6 **Re-read Text 8e. Choose and underline other extracts that would be useful as quotations in your essay.**

4.7 **Discuss your choices with a partner. Explain why you have chosen them and how you think they will be useful in completing your assignment.**
Note: When acknowledging the author in your references, you would write the following:

Gladwell, M. (2010). *The Tipping Point: How Little Things Make a Big Difference*. London: Abacus.

Study tip

It is important to use grammar and punctuation accurately when incorporating quotations into your writing. It is advisable to restrict your use of original wording to no more than a few lines.

Task 5   Planning and writing your essay

5.1   **Write your essay plan.**

5.2   **Read the essay plan of another student. Provide constructive feedback on the following points:**
- relevance of response to the task
- logical and coherent order of ideas
- effectiveness of examples
- clarity of thesis

Write the first draft of your essay.

5.3   **Read and evaluate the first draft of another student's essay.**
When you finish your first draft, exchange your draft with another student. Read your partner's draft carefully and provide feedback.

Unit and course summary

In this unit you have looked at more ways of organizing essays appropriately. You have also practised writing an essay using the comparison-and-contrast pattern.

1 **Think about the essay you wrote in Unit 8 and reflect on or discuss the questions.**

   a. How easy did you find it to plan and organize your essay?

   b. How effectively did you incorporate ideas from the texts you read into your essay?

   c. How effectively did you relate practice to theory?

   d. How useful was the peer evaluation stage of the process?

   e. Were there any language problems in your essay? How could you avoid these in the future?

2 **Think about how your writing has developed during this course. What do you feel has helped you most?**

   a. Discussions and collaboration with your fellow students. ☐

   b. Input that comes directly from your Course Book. ☐

   c. Explanations and clarification from your teacher. ☐

   d. The amount of practice you have had in writing. ☐

   e. Feedback on your writing from your tutor. ☐

   f. Working within a college or university environment. ☐

3 **Re-read the essays you have written during this course and the feedback from your teacher. Evaluate your essays as a whole for strengths and weaknesses that emerge.**

   Think about the input you have had on this course in developing your academic writing and ask yourself these questions:

   a. Is the content consistently relevant and well developed?

   b. Are the essays clearly organized, demonstrating **coherence** and cohesion?

   c. Do I manage to avoid repeated mistakes with specific language areas?

   d. Am I able to identify which areas I need to work on?

4 **Complete the table on page 93 with relevant comments in the appropriate column.**

For web resources relevant to this book, see:
www.englishforacademicstudy.com
This weblink will provide you with interesting discussions from students throughout the world, including discussions of common errors and peer editing.

academic evidence
Evidence that comes from recognized academic research or published text and is considered to be stronger and more reliable than other forms of evidence.

brainstorm
To reflect on a topic or issue and generate a large number of ideas. This can be an individual activity or a group activity in which everyone suggests as many possible ways to solve a problem or complete a task as they can.

citation
A reference to the source of an idea in someone's work. This may be an in-text reference to an author, a reference in a bibliography or footnote or a verbal reference in a talk or lecture.

coherence
Coherence of text is what enables the reader to follow the writer's train of thought. There should be coherence within sentences, between paragraphs. For example, paragraphs should flow smoothly from one to the next with the first sentence in the new paragraph linking to the one before.

complex sentence
A sentence that is made up of several clauses (main and dependent clauses). It may also include long phrases or unusual syntax and/or terminology, for example, *Crime statistics are proof positive that, with a bit of art, you can fool all the people all the time.*

concise (style)
Expressing a lot of information in a few words.

constructive criticism
Advice that is useful and intended to help someone or improve something. Constructive criticism may also involve offering possible solutions to problems.

critical reading
Reading in a way that involves questioning what the text says, what the writer is trying to do and how he/she does this.

critical thinking
Thinking critically involves the following skills: supporting your own views with a clear rationale, evaluating ideas that you hear and read, and making connections between ideas.

extended definition
This is longer and more detailed than a simple dictionary-style definition. In an extended definition there may be extended examples and/or a contrast with other similar, but distinct concepts.

genre
A type of text or art form that uses a particular style of writing or speaking. Scientific essays are a different genre from humanities essays.

manipulate
To adapt or change something (figures, statistics, facts, etc.) so that it shows what you want it to.

microskills
Skills that contribute to a larger skill (or macroskill) such as reading, writing, listening or speaking. Writing microskills include organizing and linking ideas.

paragraph leader
The first sentence in a written paragraph. The paragraph leader links to the ideas in the previous paragraph and may lead into the ideas to be developed in the next paragraph. It is a cohesive device.

paraphrase
A rewritten version of a writer's or speaker's idea, usually relating to a specific point that the writer has made, with an acknowledgement of the source.

peer evaluation
Peer evaluation takes place when a colleague or another student reads and evaluates the effectiveness of one's work. Peers are often able to suggest improvements quickly.

plagiarism
Reproducing sections of another writer's material and claiming it as your own, whether in the form of long pieces of text or short lines or phrases. This practice is unacceptable in academic writing. Any reproduction of another writer's work has to be clearly acknowledged.

process approach
An approach based on the idea that good writers go through a number of processes while composing a text before they produce their final product. It encourages the learner to go back to look at and change the text as much as he or she needs to.

source
This describes the place where information included in a text has been obtained. In academic writing, your sources will be other texts on the subject you are covering, such as journals or books.

SPSIE
An approach to problem-solving in academic life that you can use in written work. The abbreviation stands for 'situation–problems–solutions–implications–evaluation'.

terminology
Vocabulary (or terms) used in a particular field, topic or area of study. These may be technical words or terms to describe complex concepts that are specific to that topic.

thesis
A writer's point of view or position in a text is what may be referred to as his/her thesis. In order to write an evaluative project, the writer needs to develop a thesis as the starting point.

thesis statement
A statement of the writer's thesis. It is often stated in the introduction and supported by reasons in the body of the essay or presentation, and revisited in the conclusion.

topic sentence
A sentence in a paragraph that directs the ideas that are developed in the paragraph. It is important because it explains the main idea in the paragraph and helps the reader to focus on it.

Peer evaluation sheets

PEER EVALUATION SHEET: Unit 2

ESSAY: How can alternative sources of energy be harnessed effectively?

Task 1

Read your partner's draft carefully. Then read the following questions and re-read the parts of the essay which will enable you to answer them.

1.1   Introduction:
   a.   Does the essay have an introduction? ____

   b.   Does the introduction explain clearly to the reader what the topic of the essay is? If so, how has the writer achieved this?

   _____

   _____

   c.   What could the writer do to improve it?

   _____

   _____

   _____

1.2   Paragraphing:
   a.   Are the ideas in the essay grouped effectively into paragraphs? ____
   b.   If not, does the writer need to change the order of ideas? ____
   c.   Does the writer explain enough about the main idea in each paragraph to make it clear to the reader? ____

1.3   Incorporation of sources:
   a.   Has the writer included relevant ideas from the source texts to support his/her ideas? ____
   b.   If so, are these ideas successfully paraphrased and acknowledged? ____

1.4   Conclusion:
   Do you, as the reader, feel that there is a suitable conclusion which refers back to the main ideas of the essay? Why?

   _____

   _____

   _____

1.5   Additional information:
   What additional information from the texts that you have read on alternative sources of energy could be incorporated into the second draft of the essay?

   _____

   _____

   _____

Task 2

Now discuss each other's drafts. Try to comment on both the strengths and weaknesses in your partner's draft. Ask each other questions like:
■   Why did you begin as you did?
■   Why did you organize the ideas in the way you did?
■   What is the most important idea in your draft?
■   What do you mean by this point?

If points are not clear, or if the writer's main ideas are not clear, discuss these and suggest ways of making them clearer.

Task 3

Consider your partner's comments carefully. Which comments do you agree with? Why? Which comments do you disagree with? Why?

Rewrite your draft, incorporating all the improvements you have discussed and considered.

PEER EVALUATION SHEET: Unit 3

ESSAY: *Over the past 20 years, commercial influences on scientific research have become increasingly detrimental. Discuss.*

Task 1

Read your partner's draft carefully. Then read the following questions and re-read the parts of the essay which will enable you to answer them.

1.1 Introduction:

a. Does the introduction start with a general statement related to the topic and gradually become more specific? ____

b. Has the writer stated his or her viewpoint or stance in a thesis statement? ____

c. What could the writer do to improve his or her introduction?

_____

_____

1.2 Paragraphing:

a. Are the ideas in the essay grouped effectively into paragraphs? ____

b. If not, does the writer need to change the order of ideas? ____

c. Does each paragraph have a paragraph leader which tells the reader what the main idea of the paragraph is? ____

d. What is the function of each paragraph leader?

_____

_____

e. Does the writer explain enough about the main idea in each paragraph to make it clear to the reader? ____

f. If not, does the writer need to add further information or examples?

_____

_____

g. Does the writer need to remove unnecessary information?

_____

_____

1.3 Argument:

a. Is the writer's argument clear throughout the essay? ____

b. Is the writer's argument well supported with evidence? ____

c. Has the writer given opposing viewpoints? ____

d. Does the writer's argument convince you? ____

1.4 Incorporation of sources:

a. Has the writer successfully incorporated ideas from his/her sources into the essay? ____

b. Has the writer *commented* on these ideas, showing they have thought about them critically? ____

1.5 Conclusion:

Do you feel, as the reader, that there is a suitable conclusion to the essay which refers back to the main ideas of the essay?

_____

_____

_____

Task 2

Now discuss each other's drafts. Try to comment on both the strengths and weaknesses in your partner's draft.

Task 3

Consider your partner's comments carefully. Which comments do you agree with? Why? Which comments do you disagree with? Why?

Rewrite your draft, incorporating all the improvements you have discussed and considered.

PEER EVALUATION SHEET: Unit 5

ESSAY: There are many threats to global food supplies. Explain the problem, identify possible solutions, and assess the implications of implementing these solutions.

Task 1

Read your partner's draft carefully. Then read the following questions and re-read the parts of the essay which will enable you to answer them.

1.1 Introduction:

a. Does the introduction start with a general statement related to the topic and gradually become more specific? ____

b. Has the writer stated his or her viewpoint or stance in a thesis statement? ____

c. What could the writer do to improve his/her introduction?

_____

_____

1.2 Paragraphing and organization:

a. Are the ideas in the essay grouped effectively into paragraphs? ____

b. If not, does the writer need to change the order of ideas? ____

c. Does each paragraph have a paragraph leader which tells the reader what the main idea of the paragraph is? ____

d. What is the function of each paragraph leader?

_____

_____

e. Does the writer explain enough about the main idea in each paragraph to make it clear to the reader? ____

f. If not, does the writer need to add further information or examples? ____

g. Does the writer need to remove unnecessary information? ____

h. Does each paragraph have a concluding sentence which appropriately ends the paragraph? ____

i. Find two concluding sentences and write down what you think their function is.

_____

_____

_____

_____

1.3 Incorporation of sources:

a. Is information from the text appropriately incorporated and paraphrased? ____

b. If not, what should the writer do to improve it?

_____

_____

c. Underline two examples where information has been incorporated from the text.

d. Are sources of information appropriately acknowledged?

1.4 Conclusion:

a. Does the essay have an appropriate conclusion? ____

b. What is the particular function of the conclusion?

_____

_____

c. What could the writer do to improve it?

_____

_____

Task 2

Now discuss each other's drafts. Try to comment on both the strengths and weaknesses in your partner's draft.

Task 3

Consider your partner's comments carefully. Which comments do you agree with? Why? Which comments do you disagree with? Why?

Rewrite your draft, incorporating all the improvements you have discussed and considered.

PEER EVALUATION SHEET: Unit 6

ESSAY: To what extent does human resource management need to play a formal role in companies?

Task 1

Read your partner's draft carefully. Then read the following questions and re-read the parts of the essay which will enable you to answer them.

1.1   Introduction:

a. Does the introduction start with a general statement related to the topic and gradually become more specific? ____

b. Has the writer stated his or her viewpoint or stance in a thesis statement ____

c. What could the writer do to improve his/her introduction?

_____

_____

1.2   Definitions:

a. Underline any definitions of important words or expressions that the writer has made.

b. Has the writer used appropriate language in his/her definitions? ____

c. If the writer has not included any definitions, do you think he/she should have? If so, what words should have been defined?

_____

_____

1.3   Paragraphing:

a. Are the ideas in the essay grouped effectively into paragraphs? ____

b. If not, does the writer need to change the order of ideas? ____

c. Does each paragraph have a paragraph leader which tells the reader what the main idea of the paragraph is? ____

d. What is the function of each paragraph leader?

_____

_____

e. Does the writer explain enough about the main idea in each paragraph to make it clear to the reader? ____

f. If not, does the writer need to add further information or examples? ____

g. If the writer has added support to his/her main idea, how has he/she done this?

_____

_____

h. Does the writer need to remove unnecessary information? ____

i. Does each paragraph have a concluding sentence which appropriately ends the paragraph? ____

j. Find two concluding sentences and write down what you think their function is.

_____

_____

1.4   Conclusion:

a. Does the essay have an appropriate conclusion? ____

b. What is the particular function of the conclusion?

_____

_____

c. What could the writer do to improve it?

_____

_____

Task 2

Now discuss each other's drafts. Try to comment on both the strengths and weaknesses in your partner's draft.

Task 3

Consider your partner's comments carefully. Which comments do you agree with? Why? Which comments do you disagree with? Why?

Rewrite your draft, incorporating all the improvements you have discussed and considered.

ESSAY: The fashion industry poses a serious threat to the environment. A higher level of sustainability in materials production is the key solution. Discuss.

Task 1

Read your partner's draft carefully. Then read the following questions and re-read the parts of the essay which will enable you to answer them.

1.1 Introduction:

a. Does the introduction start with a general statement related to the topic and gradually become more specific? ___

b. Is there a clear thesis statement which says what the essay will be about and gives the writer's viewpoint or stance? ___

c. Does the essay explain what the introduction said it would? ___

d. What could the writer do to improve it?

_____

_____

1.2 Definitions:

a. Has the writer used appropriate language in his/her definitions? ___

b. If the writer has not included any definitions, do you think he/she should have? ___

c. If so, what words should have been defined?

_____

_____

1.3 Overall organization:

a. What pattern of organization has the author used?

_____

_____

b. Is it clear that the writer is writing about cause and effect/SPSIE in part of the essay? ___

c. How could the writer improve his/her overall structure?

_____

_____

1.4 Paragraphing:

a. Are the ideas in the essay grouped effectively into paragraphs?

b. If not, does the writer need to change the order of ideas? ___

c. Does each paragraph have a paragraph leader? ___

d. If the writer has added support to his/her main idea, how has he/she done this?

_____

_____

e. If not, does the writer need to add further information or examples? ___

f. Does the writer need to remove unnecessary information? ___

g. Does each paragraph have a concluding sentence which appropriately ends the paragraph? ___

1.5 Incorporation of sources:

a. Is information from the text appropriately incorporated? ___

b. If not, what should the writer do?

_____

_____

c. Underline two examples where information has been incorporated.

1.6 Conclusion:

a. Does the essay have an appropriate conclusion? ___

b. What is the particular function of the conclusion?

_____

_____

c. What could the writer do to improve it?

_____

_____

Task 2

Now discuss each other's drafts. Try to comment on both the strengths and weaknesses in your partner's draft.

Task 3

Consider your partner's comments carefully. Rewrite your draft, incorporating all the improvements you have discussed and considered.

PEER EVALUATION SHEET: Unit 8

ESSAY: Compare and contrast the role of Innovators and Early Adopters with the role of the Early Majority in achieving commercial success. Relate your answer to Gladwell's theory of the Tipping Point.

Task 1

Read your partner's draft carefully. Then read the following questions and re-read the parts of the essay which will enable you to answer them. (As you have now followed this procedure for five units, the guidance for this final one has been reduced.)

1.1 Introduction:
a. Bearing in mind what you have learnt about introductions, what could the writer do to improve it?

_____

_____

_____

1.2 Definitions:
a. Has the writer used enough definitions and used appropriate language when defining them? ____
b. What could the writer do to improve their use of definitions?

_____

_____

_____

_____

1.3 Overall organization:
a. What pattern of organization has the author used?

_____

b. Has the writer used a horizontal or vertical pattern where he/she compares and contrasts? ____
c. How could the writer improve his/her overall structure?

_____

_____

_____

_____

1.4 Paragraphing:
a. Are the ideas in the essay grouped effectively into paragraphs? ____

b. Comment on the structure of the paragraphs in terms of what you have learnt during the course.

_____

_____

_____

_____

1.5 Incorporation of sources:
a. Is information used from the text appropriately incorporated? ____
b. If not, what should the writer do?

_____

_____

c. Are there any examples of direct quotes? Are these appropriately formatted? ____

1.6 Conclusion:
a. Does the essay have an appropriate conclusion? ____
b. What is the function of the conclusion?

_____

_____

_____

c. What could the writer do to improve it?

_____

_____

_____

Task 2

Now discuss each other's drafts. Try to comment on both the strengths and weaknesses in your partner's draft.

Task 3

Consider your partner's comments carefully. Rewrite your draft, incorporating all the improvements you have discussed and considered.

Appendix: Assessing my progress

In this section, you will assess the progress in your academic writing that you have made so far on this course, by evaluating the essays you have written and deciding on your strengths and weaknesses.

1.1 **Thinking about the input that you have had on this course on developing your academic writing, re-read your essays and the feedback that the teacher has given you. Look for strengths and weaknesses that occur in more than one essay. Ask yourself these questions:**

- Is the content in my essays consistently relevant and well developed?
- Do I have consistent problems with organization?
- Do I make repeated mistakes with certain language areas?
- If so, can I identify exactly which areas I need to work on (e.g., agreement of subject and verb; present perfect tense)?

1.2 **Complete the table on page 93 with relevant comments in the appropriate columns.**

1.3 **What actions are you going to take to ensure you continue to develop your academic writing skills?**

_____

_____

_____

_____

_____

_____

_____

_____

_____

_____

_____

_____

_____

My progress in academic writing   Name: _____

	What I've been taught and can apply in my essays	What I've been taught but have difficulty in applying in my essays	Overall strengths	Overall weaknesses	My main areas to focus on in the future
Task achievement (relating the essay to the title or topic, and overall completion of essay)					
Organization					
Content					
Language					